THE MAN WHO SHOOK MOUNTAINS
In the footsteps of my ancestors

LESLEY MOFOKENG

Jonathan Ball Publishers
JOHANNESBURG • CAPE TOWN

All rights reserved.
No part of this publication may be reproduced or transmitted, in any form or by any means, without prior permission from the publisher or copyright holder.

© Text Lesley Mofokeng 2023
© Published edition 2023 Jonathan Ball Publishers

Originally published in South Africa in 2023 by
JONATHAN BALL PUBLISHERS
A division of Media24 (Pty) Ltd
PO Box 33977
Jeppestown
2043

ISBN 978-1-77619-251-9
ebook ISBN 978-1-77619-252-6

Every effort has been made to trace the copyright holders and to obtain their permission for the use of copyright material. The publishers apologise for any errors or omissions and would be grateful to be notified of any corrections that should be incorporated in future editions of this book.

www.jonathanball.co.za
www.twitter.com/JonathanBallPub
www.facebook.com/JonathanBallPublishers

Cover by Sean Robertson
Design and typesetting by Melanie Kriel
Set in 10/15.5pt PT Serif

This book is dedicated to my children Mahali Leseli and Chapatso Kgosi, and to the memory of my grandparents Mongangane and Mahadi, of my father Moses, of my cousin Limpho Masithela, and of my friend Thapelo Molekwa.

Moruti wa Sekuta (Evangelist on a Scooter)
by Nkosinathi Quwe (2020)

Contents

	Author's note	vii
	Preface	ix
1	Return to innocence	1
2	The land of mountains and flowing rivers	13
3	Marabi in Magogogong	24
4	Coming of age	35
5	1625 Shelters Number 2, Orlando	41
6	Once a Pirate, always a Pirate	49
7	The making of an evangelist	53
8	In the lucky lake	66
9	Construction site	74
10	The making of a leader	87
11	The 'luck' in Gelukspan	103
12	Family reflections	108
13	The wind beneath his wings	116
14	The Rollands of Beersheba	129
15	The blood of Beersheba	138
16	The reckoning	143
17	The church	149

18	The French connection and the Boer influence	158
19	Is 'theft' the charge?	180
20	We shall sing a new song	186
21	Shaking mountains for answers	197
	Acknowledgements	210
	Bibliography	215
	Index	222
	About the author	226

Author's note

The figure of my grandfather, Mongangane Wilfred Mofokeng, was a constant in my life for over 32 years. He lived a long life of service, dedication and conscientious effort towards making the lives of others better. My enduring earliest memory of him was when I had to go to school in Grade 1 and how he was always up first in the kitchen to prepare my lunchbox, which would more often than not be boiled eggs and bread. It became a staple and also a butt of jokes in the class whenever anyone caught a whiff of a foul smell wafting in the air. Then there was my equally hardworking grandmother who stood by him side by side. She had the most influence in how I view the world and always had something to say about everything. All I wanted was to sit at her feet and listen to what she had to say. She was a disciplinarian and comedian in equal measure.

This book is essentially telling their story from a perspective of their grandchild. But it steps beyond the walls of our house in Gelukspan, a rural settlement in the district of Ditsobotla (Lichtenburg), North West. It goes to Gauteng, Free State, Lesotho and France. It's a historical record of one South African family and a descendant seeking to find understanding of his place in an ever-changing society.

In writing history, I retained the original spellings of names, places and things that were written differently at that time to reflect the period. Current names are reflected as such – for example, Mafeking becomes Mahikeng where I am referring to the place in the present. Where there are conflicting spellings, I have considered the options and chosen the spelling that seems best for me, erring on the side of consistency within the manuscript. I accept that others might differ with me on my choices.

I also decided to denote race by using capitals. It was important for me to do so in honour of the Black African people who came before me. This is also to highlight the importance placed on race during the days of segregation.

I have to make a disclaimer regarding the translations contained in this book. Due to the idiomatic nature of hymns that were composed some 190 years ago, my translations are approximations. I attempted to be as literal as possible, but I suspect someone else might have a different interpretation.

Preface

This book was birthed in the Master's class at Wits University where I first presented the idea of telling the story of my late grandfather, Mongangane Wilfred Mofokeng, as part of a long-form, non-fiction, narrative journalism project.

I initially titled it *Moruti wa Sekuta* – The Evangelist on a Scooter – and I set off to tell the colourful life of a man who has had a great impact and influence on my life. Its present title, *The Man Who Shook Mountains*, is drawn from the words of Seetso Moremong, whom I interviewed along with many others. As a boy who had grown up in Bapong village in what is today the North West province, Moremong remembered my grandfather's legendary scooter kicking up the white dust as he buzzed in and around the Gelukspan area to minister to his congregants. Moremong also recalled Mongangane's moving and powerful sermons, which he said were 'capable of shaking mountains ... with his full and loud voice calling on Jehovah'.

'Ntate Mofokeng,' he told me, 'pulled people towards God with the great and rare talent of a motivator.'

The title of my book is also, however, a testament to the journeys I took in search of my identity, from the mountains of the eastern Free State to Lesotho, where the echoes of my ancestors and chants of years gone by filled me with a sense of completeness.

Biography, memoir, history, health, politics, theology and 'missiology' – which is the study of missions and their methods –

are woven together in this text. I seek to shed light on my subject – my grandfather – and the impact of his presence and evangelism in the communities he worked in.

I realised along the way how important it is that this story is written, especially since the documented records from the church, the hospital and the schools Mongangane worked in cannot be found. The new minister at Gelukspan church, Reverend Shadrack Moepeng, said he inherited no records after the upheavals that beset the church during the time of the minister who followed Mongangane. Nothing was handed over to him. Nor did the hospital have any records dating back to his time. The same goes for the schools.

Save for a few photographs that survived the passage of time and now stand as evidence of his life's work, my grandfather's remarkable story has largely been conveyed orally. To write it up is to formalise it and to add it to the written histories of this country. I came to see this as an important undertaking, not only for my own understanding of my place in my family's history, but to add to a wider undertaking of social comprehension of our complex past.

* * *

I start the book by retracing Mongangane's steps and reconstruct his story by revisiting what's left of what he built some 70 years ago. The narration includes flashbacks to his life back then and how things at Gelukspan are currently in a state of neglect and disrepair.

The attention then shifts to Germiston and Johannesburg of the 1930s, the politics of the time and Black life under oppression. Mongangane followed the popular migration trail to the city of gold, which would be home to the young Mofokeng family for about a decade. I delve into life in a new township called Orlando in Soweto. Mongangane's own politicisation and awakening is also explored. Sport became an ally both in the struggle against oppression and also in maintaining sanity for Black men (and women) on the Reef.

At the halfway mark of his life, Mongangane, aged about 40, turned to the church and swapped his unskilled labourer overalls for the collar as he became an evangelist. Here I unpack the Nederduitse Gereformeerde Kerk (colloquially known as the NG Kerk and in English as the Dutch Reformed Church) and its controversial history and contribution towards the promotion of apartheid. I question how my grandfather became an agent of an institution that aimed to oppress his own freedom.

I settle on a cattle outpost called Gelukspan. It's 1952, and the grand project of apartheid begins to sink its teeth into South African society. Black people are being evicted from the cities and townships to live in the reserves. We see a new dynamic as villages called reserves and resettlements – also known as Trusts – spring up. This is where the ingenuity of Mongangane came into play as he set out to build a community and contribute towards its members' spiritual, physical and educational wellbeing.

In the chapter following that, I focus on Mahadi, Mongangane's wife, who was an influential player in his story. She ran the Mofokeng household meticulously and supported Mongangane in remarkable ways well worth documenting, while also being an indomitable force of economic plans and ideas.

After sketching the lives of my grandparents, I drill down into the politics and history of the NG Kerk and its Black constituency. I journey to the mission station of Beersheba, a place which marked a turning point in the journey of a church that was brought to South Africa by French missionaries led by Eugene Casalis, Thomas Arbousset and Constand Gosselin.

The French influence remained in the name Kereke ya Fora – Church of the French. I wanted to know why the Dutch church, which my family was connected to, was still associated in name with the French, and I try to find out how that happened.

I journey into present-day Lesotho in search of answers and make startling connections with my beginning. Standing on top of Thaba Bosiu and bowing my head at the tomb of King Moshoeshoe, the founder to the Basotho nation, and drinking from *seliba sa 'MaMohato* (the well of 'MaMohato) brought history physically close to me.

* * *

Mongangane was a man of his time, as this story will reveal. We see him dance to the rhythm of the most pivotal periods of his life that are punctuated by laws, statutes and events of significant national importance. This story celebrates his spirit, what he stood for and how he charted a new path for himself and for his family given the circumstances he found himself in and the challenges he faced. People who knew him, people who worked for him or under him or beside him, paint a picture of that time for us, a time that seems far in years, but is still within living memory.

This is a South African story of an unsung hero, a man forgotten by history – though not by me, nor by the people who knew and respected him – and whose legacy could easily go unacknowledged.

Mongangane would have been 108 years old in 2022. Many of the people I interviewed were in their 70s and 80s and it was not easy for them to reach deep into the wells of their memories. Some of the facts had to be double- and triple-checked. In the end, sometimes I had to make a leap of imagination to reach a point of agreement or simply lay out the contradictory facts. That, though, is part of the telling a 95-year-long unrecorded life of a servant of the people. What seems beyond dispute is that it's on Mongangane's back that Gelukspan stands to this day.

* * *

Writing this book, it must be noted, is – apart from an attempt to inscribe an important personal history – in many ways the fulfilment of a prophecy.

My grandfather's wish was for me to study at Wits University after matric, but with financial constraints I stayed on in Mafikeng, where I grew up, and went to North West University. I imagine that, as a labourer working in Johannesburg and seeing the sprawling Wits University develop – and seeing the likes of Nelson Mandela studying there and witnessing the prestige of the university rise in the years that followed – it remained his wish that his children or grandchildren would study there.

It is profound for me that I earned my Master's degree from Wits University, using his life story as my research project, 11 years after he rested in the Lord.

I hope that I have made him proud that his wish for me came to pass.

1
Return to innocence

Author Lesley Mofokeng stands in the church
his grandfather built in 1958. PHOTO: FAMILY ALBUM

Gelukspan, North West, December 2019

Today I walked into a church my grandfather built in 1958. It was like 1982 all over again at my grandparents' lively mission house. Sunday morning ... breakfast on the table, then a hurried walk to Sunday School. Standing there, I was overwhelmed with emotion and memories. I was stepping back in time.

The church is an imposing structure with the trademark NG Kerk steeple mounted by a cock that – at least to my eyes, when I was a child – looked like it reached up past the clouds to the blue sky. Back then, the wooden benches, wooden floor and the elegant chandelier gave it a dignified touch. The large champagne-coloured stained-glass windows added an ethereal, other-worldly feel to it.

This building was, in my childhood, a majestic landmark, jutting out of the uninspiring platteland of Gelukspan in the Lichtenburg district in North West. I believed sincerely and without any doubt that it was indeed the house of God.

The last time I was here was in December 1984 for my grandparents' farewell ceremony. A memory etched in my mind is that of my weeping grandmother, too emotional to contain the sadness of leaving a congregation she worked in for 32 years and what had become home not only to her, but to generations of her descendants.

The two of them, Mongangane and Mahadi, sat by the pulpit in front of the congregation one last time as the flock paid their respects and gave them modest farewell gifts.

The whole affair seemed rushed to me. It did not fit the stature of my grandparents. I expected bigger crowds and even bigger dignitaries – important people that had worked with them for over three decades.

Here they were now, getting ready for the uncertainty of retirement, and the prospect seemed too much for my grandmother to bear. I wanted to reach out to her, to comfort her, but with church rules and protocol, I had to sit still in the Sunday School section and helplessly watch her pain.

* * *

Now, in 2019, 35 years after my grandparents' retirement, and a few nights before Christmas, the church is empty as we wait outside and wander around the premises.

My two children, Mahali and Chapatso, are with me on this momentous trip retracing our family roots. So is my cousin Mpho, whom everyone calls Prof, and his wife, Nqobile, and their three girls.

We can peep through windows since the stained glass has been replaced by regular glass. The wooden benches and wooden flooring are gone.

The great-grandchildren of Mongangane Mofokeng visit their forebear's church. PHOTO: AUTHOR

A friendly woman, identifying herself only as Mrs Koko, keeper of the church keys, emerges to fling open the doors and to welcome us. She immediately recognises us as the grandchildren of Mofokeng and her face lights up. She opens up her arms to hug us and wastes no time telling us how great our grandfather was and about his contribution in making the lives of the people in Gelukspan better.

I point out to her that his name does not appear on the church stone. The White dominee's name – TI Ferreira – is there.

Mrs Koko agrees that Mongangane Mofokeng's name ought to be there too. But my grandfather's name is not immortalised on any stone. There is nothing that formally acknowledges his physical, mental and spiritual work in the church, the hospital, the schools and the community of Gelukspan.

We walk into the church and nostalgia is a shock like a slap across the face.

Music and church hymns are an important part of my own life and my relationship with spirituality. When I was young, the mellifluous voices of the choir of youngsters living with disabilities from Tlamelang Special School filled this space. The choir was something of a legend in school music competitions under the baton of Mistress Dorothy Morapedi, picking up all the silverware and leaving their competitors devastated.

I remember so well their renditions of *Ke Na Le Molisa* (I Have a Shepherd), *Bophelo ke Wena Fela* (You, Alone, Give Us Life), *Jesu Motswalle Ya Nkileng* (What a Friend We Have in Jesus) and *Ha Le Mpotsa Tshepo Ya Ka* (If You Ask Me Where My Hope Comes From), but also the popular choruses they sang for us.

Now, today, all I can hear is the echo of our own voices reverberating throughout the crumbling structure as we peer and peek into all the nooks and corners of the over 60-year-old building.

Mrs Koko calls to us from the *konsistorie* (the backroom of the church reserved for the minister and the church council). She shows us the exact utensils our grandfather used for *selallo* (holy communion). The wooden tot dispenser, the tithing bowl, the baptismal stand. They are still in use, she says, and they hold a sentimental place in the hearts of those who witnessed the great work of Mongangane.

Mrs Koko shows the utensils used by Mongangane Mofokeng in the years he was the evangelist of the Gelukspan church. PHOTO: AUTHOR

What she is demonstrating flushes out another memory: standing here in the same *konsistorie* as a curious six-year-old, watching my grandfather count the stock for holy communion. I would beg him to share the communion wine with me.

'Just a taste,' I would implore.

Ever the disciplinarian, he would flatly refuse and reprimand me, '*He-e, o ngwana, ha se dintho tsa hao tse*' ('No, you're a child, this is not for you'), but he would offer me two cubes of the communion bread to shush me. Such were the privileges of being brought up by a preacher man.

He always locked away the communion wine before we left for home. I promised myself that one day I would devise a plan to steal the key and help myself to copious amounts of this red drink that seems to be loved by the older members of the congregation. That scheme never came to pass.

* * *

The wooden flooring has been replaced by tiles and the wooden benches have made way for black plastic chairs. The ceiling is peeling, and it is cracking as though it's about to give in but, by faith, is holding on for dear life. The pulpit, remarkably, has remained intact. The iconic, but faded, *Modimo o Lerato* (God is Love) church *lesela* (cloth) still hangs there. It used to be a deep, strong colour, but it has had one too many washes and has become more orange than blood-of-lamb red. The gold tassels have all disintegrated. Not a single strand has survived the years.

We gather around in the well on the church near the pulpit, and Mrs Koko says a prayer, thanking God for bringing us together and wishing us well as we depart – this after Nqobile led the small congregation in the rendition of the popular hymn *Re Ya Ho Boka Morena* (We Praise You Lord).

We file out of the church feeling fulfilled. The small rituals, the words, the song, the prayer – it is as though we have just witnessed a powerful sermon. We had felt the presence of our grandfather's spirit, despite the dilapidation and the silence.

* * *

We head towards the hospital complex. This place too, is an important part of Mongangane's story in Gelukspan.

We walk through the corridors – past the outpatient department, medical wards, TB wards, administration block – and out on to the cobbled walkway to the now-deserted nurses' home. The once-noisy handicrafts workshop with machines whirring and burring away is as silent as a haunted old house.

The hall, which could seat over 500 people, and which had looked absolutely massive to my young eyes, is in a state of disrepair. There are no signs of its previous life anywhere. Today, the spiders in the cosy homes of their cobwebs here would laugh in my face if I told them about the beauty pageants that were held on that stage; the concerts, the music and dance competitions that electrified the place and whipped revellers into a frenzy.

Perhaps the most enduring memory of the hall is of the Good Friday services that were held there and the night vigils over the holy weekend.

The hall would be filled to capacity in a Mecca-like – okay, make that Moria-like – gathering of the faithful from all the villages around Gelukspan, ferried by trucks, lorries, tractors and even horse- and donkey-drawn carts.

The services had become so popular that families and relatives would travel from as far as Johannesburg and Pretoria to take part. On Friday, beasts – usually a cow and a few sheep – would be slaughtered. Pots of *ting* (sour sorghum porridge), pap and samp would be on the braziers as excitement mounted.

The Saturday service was heralded by pomp and ceremony.

A long procession of church elders and deacons draped in their *manele* (coats with tails) would file into the hall and fill up the stage. The spectacle was not unlike a university graduation ceremony. It had real gravitas. The last to walk in would be my grandfather and the resident minister. After the opening sermon, my grandmother and Mejuffrou, as she was generally known, would take over the programme with the clothing ceremony.

My grandmother and Mejuffrou Ferreira, wife of the Afrikaans minister who served with my grandparents in the 50s and 60s, would undertake the ceremony of clothing the new members of the church from the ministries of Mokgatlo wa Bacha ba BaKreste (MBB) for the young, and Christelike Vroue Vereeniging (CVV) for the older women.

How it worked was that new members came dressed in black long-sleeve collarless jackets, skirts, stockings and shoes. Then my grandmother and Mejuffrou would place the white circular collar on their shoulders and hold it in place with a branded pin. Then they would place the black woollen beret on the women's heads.

I gleaned from writing by the Late Reverend Dr Mary-Anne Plaatjies-van Huffel, moderator of the General Synod, that the symbolism of the uniform is as follows: the beret, jacket, skirt, shoes and stockings are black to indicate the sinful nature of human beings that can only be washed by the blood of Jesus Christ. The white collar is a symbol of Jesus having washed our sins away.

The five buttons on the jacket symbolise the five areas where Jesus was stabbed while on the cross. These are his hands, feet, side, back and head. The two pockets of the jacket indicate that Christian women should be peacemakers and keep their swords in their sheaths, just as Jesus instructed Peter when Jesus was captured. The beret is worn because the Bible instructs women to pray with a hat on.

The women are encouraged to shun make up and jewellery when wearing church uniform. This is to allow their beauty to come from within and for them to be known for their good deeds. The uniform is a symbol of simplicity, minimalism, plainness and a devotion to Jesus. It is meant to break boundaries between rich and poor members, those who can afford expensive clothes and jewellery and those who cannot.

The uniform is optional. Women are not obliged to be robed, and to be robed one has to undergo a year-long trial.

No fewer than 50 new members would receive the new uniform every Good Friday weekend.

* * *

The clothing ceremony would be followed by a highly charged revival that would be hosted overnight. Members would take turns at this to preach and to share the Word.

On Sunday morning, the hall would be filled once more as the holy communion was shared. The holy weekend was coming to a close and congregants were about to embark on their long journeys back home.

With the gathering of so many people under one roof, tragedy was bound to strike sooner or later.

One year, a mother left her infant sleeping peacefully on the grass under a tree. It had been brought to be baptised. A tractor driver, coming to fetch members, bumped over something, probably thinking it was a rock.

Horror of horrors. The mother was hospitalised for several days after her baby was crushed to death. The shock and trauma were overwhelming.

I sometimes wonder if that family ever recovered from the ordeal.

* * *

Looking at this hall now in its dilapidated state, you might agree with the resident spiders that I'm probably telling a fable.

The neglected hall is falling apart. PHOTO: AUTHOR

Next on our list of places to visit is the house where my grandparents lived. It's big structure by most people's standards but not much in the way of imagination and architecture. It looks quite a lot like an unsliced loaf of white bread.

This is where I grew up.

And a lot has changed.

The big peach tree at the front of the house has been uprooted. The happy noise that always hung in the air around this yard and this house is silent now. There used to be a lot of comings and goings as people queued to buy the buns my grandmother made. There was always a cock wreaking havoc among the chickens, and the delightful screams and squeals of playful children running around.

Once a busy community node, the Mofokeng house looks forlorn and has lost its charm. PHOTO: AUTHOR

My grandfather had a study where he prepared for his sermons. It doubled up as a library, which housed his collection of Christian books that he used as reference and that he consulted to deepen his understanding of the scriptures.

The house is locked. The current minister is on leave and there is no access for us, but we don't allow this to make us feel despondent. Just as many memories were made outside this house as were made inside. We used to eat unripe peaches from the small backyard tree and get diarrhoea, for instance. Or we pitted the cocks against each other for the brutal blood sport of cockfighting.

Shameful.

There are no chickens here now, but we help ourselves to a few unripe peaches for old time's sake.

As we drive out of the hospital complex, we notice that the

orchard that lined the fence has disappeared. Here we got endless supplies of peaches, apricots, pears, naartjies and pomegranates – all gone now.

We wave at the friendly security guard who checks every car leaving and entering the place.

My cousin and I, who are most closely bound to this place, are heavy with nostalgia and a sense of the time we will never return to.

2
The land of mountains and flowing rivers

FAMILY TREE

- Moojane born in Matlakeng c. 1690
- Moojane born in Malatsi c. 1710
- Koeema born in Malatsi c. 1730
- Tsietso born in Malatsi c. 1750
- Nkejane born in Malatsi c. 1770
- Tshehlo born c. 1780 and died before June 1847
- Nanau born c. 1790 (could be Chapatso's father)
- Chapatso born in Madraereng c. 1830

Sepenya born in Madraereng c. 1873	Themere born in Madraereng c. 1875	Tontshi born in Madraereng c. 1877
Montlha born in Madraereng c. 1879	Makuoe born in Madraereng c. 1881	Takatso born in Madraereng c. 1884

Mongangane born in Madraereng c. 1914

Jerry	Takatso	Ephraim	Bernard	Moses	Tshidiso
Thabang, Teboho and Nthabiseng	Mpho, Tsenolo and Tiisetso	Rasebopela, Sabata and Selloane	Lerato, Mmuso and Teboho	Thabiso, Lesley and Palesa	Dimakatso and Dipolelo

The story goes that we are Egyptians, descendants of the ancient Pharaoh, the people of the Nile who came far south. Somewhere along the line, we became Matebele, who were later assimilated into Bafokeng.

While most Bafokeng regard the rabbit as their totem, my clan does not. We identify as the people of the dew – the owners of the land and of life itself. Animals walk on dew at the break of dawn and draw life from the moist grass and the sweet waters of the dew.

In the days of Shaka, the king of AmaZulu, when warriors planned to attack BaMoojane and BaTshele, Lesotho was known as 'Lesotho of Nkejane'. Nkejane was renowned for his prowess on the battlefield and became a legend in foreign lands. His son, Tshehlo, was also a gallant warrior in the wars of those times in the late 1700s.

One of the protestant missionaries who came to South Africa to work among the Basotho was Frederic Ellenberger from Switzerland. He wrote substantially about my BaMoojane ancestors among other Basotho clans and heroes. He noted that there was little record of the early history of the BaMoojane. He adds that according to Azariel Sekese, the earliest Mosotho historian, BaMoojane were originally Matebele, and that they were assimilated in to the Bafokeng clan. 'On their arrival,' he says, 'they were only boys of Tseana.' Tseana was one of the fathers of BaMoojane, an ancestor of the family.

When they grew up, they took wives and tried, without success, to pass themselves off as Bafokeng. At the time of the death of Ratlali – that is to say, about the year 1690 – 'they were at Matlakeng on the left bank of the Caledon, claiming to belong to Mahlatsana, younger brother of Mahlatsi,' says Sekese, quoted by Ellenberger, 'but then the Mahlatsi are Makhoakhoa, and therefore Bakuena.'

After many years in Lesotho they became Basotho, taking up the language, laws and customs.

An article in *Leselinyana la Lesotho* – a newspaper founded by Adolphe Mabille of the Paris Evangelical Mission Society (PEMS) in 1863 – authored by the same Sekese who was quoted in Ellenberger's book, puts it differently. It says the BaMoojane lived in 'Makalane with the Makhoakhoa as their neighbours. In Matlakeng, lived BaMakhoakhoa, and in Kubetu were BaTshele.

From Matlakeng they went to 'Malatsi, where they joined the Bakhatla somewhere around the year 1720. They remained there for several generations, and the following were born there: Kueeme, son of Moojane; Tsietso, son of Kueeme; Nkejane, son of Tsietso; and Tshehlo, son of Nkejane.

Their life there was without incident, and passed in agricultural pursuits, so that they increased considerably. But Tshehlo became famous for his bravery – and for the manner of his death, as we shall see later – for while they were all living with the Bakhatla they were invaded by Letuka Hlabeli, known as one of the powerful Basotho warriors. Being too weak to resist, Tshehlo submitted to Letuka. This was, for BaMoojane, the beginning of the Difaqane, a historical period lasting between one and three decades, depending on which sources are used, during which military conflict and migration happened across southern Africa. From that time forward their history is included in that of that terrible period.

In his chapter on invasions and Difaqane, Ellenberger relates the troubles that befell Basotho. He says the Drakensberg mountains that had long been thought of as a fort against raids proved not to be one. The Batlokoa and Masopha had raided Bafokeng of Mabula and Moshoeshoe.

Ellenberger records that the Bafokeng, on this occasion, were driven from their homes, and after a brief sojourn with the Ramaiyane near Fouriesburg, formed themselves into bands of robbers, trekking about the country with their women, children and cattle, and robbing and murdering those who were not strong enough to resist. Their chiefs were Ntabenyane, son of Tseele, and Letuka, son of Hlabeli.

Nkejane and Tshehlo, along with Bamaiyane who lived in Mautse and was too weak to resist, joined the raiders. Letuka, with his ranks filled by the new reinforcements, attacked the Bamaiyane of Futhane, who had formerly harboured him, destroying everything they had. It is said that he drove them to cannibalism.

At this time, Tshehlo lived between Mautse, in the picturesque Eastern Free State with views to the majestic mountains, and what was called Brindisi Drift. His father, Nkejane, meanwhile lived on the slopes of Mautse with a few followers. After the attack on the Bamaiyane they returned to these places, and the Bafokeng of Mabula settled near them on the banks of what Ellenberger calls the Brandwater river.

Ellenberger said certain of the Bafokeng – namely Mokiba and the sons of Masekoane from Botha-Bothe – came and joined those of Mabula. They soon found that they were in bad company and left secretly with all that they had brought. They were so impoverished that they had to beg leave from Moshoeshoe to reap the self-sown grain from his fields that no one else could lay claim to. But Ntabenyane and Letuka continued raiding. They attacked Morallana, another Mofokeng who lived at Hlakoli, just by Brindisi Drift and, after scattering his people, captured his cattle.

Ellenberger documented the conversation between Letuka and Tshehlo after this adventure thus: 'Letuka said to Tshehlo, who had assisted him, "Tell me, Tshehlo, you know the land, whom shall we raid now?" Tshehlo answered, "Chief, there is no one. Beyond these hills lives Mokhachane, who is a friend of mine, and he who desires to kill him must kill me also." This spoke volumes of the loyalty and admiration Tshehlo had for the father of Moshoeshoe.'

Letuka seemed happy with the response from Tshehlo, but Tshehlo did not trust him, so he sent a warning with one of his messengers to King Moshoeshoe, and advised him to send a peace offering to Letuka.

Moshoeshoe indeed sent four cows to Letuka. Notwithstanding the peace offering, Letuka attacked Mokiba and captured the cattle of Mokiba. Two of the women with them were Mathebetoa, who became the mother of Matsoso, and Mankejane, who became the mother of Khotso. This defeat broke up this band of robbers. Some joined Tshehlo and others later on made their submission to Moshoeshoe.

Ellenberger said the friendship between Moshoeshoe and Tshehlo was solidified when Tshehlo was instrumental in recovering certain cattle that had been stolen from Moshoeshoe in a separate incident before Letuka came into picture.

This outbreak of hostility between the Bafokeng and Mabula ended here. It is not connected with the events that caused the great Lifaqane, but it was the outcome of a raid from beyond the Drakensberg, and therefore has to be recorded.

* * *

It is unanimous that I am a descendant of Moojane (sometimes written as Mohojane) who can be traced back to 1600, half a century before the White man set foot here.

Tshehlo settled on top of Mount Kgoele also known as *Die Tafelberg van die Vrystaat* because of its flat top, reminiscent of the famous Table Mountain in Cape Town. You can find it on the way from present-day Senekal to Paul Roux. Those who have summitted

Kgoele have told of remnants they have found, evidence of times gone by. Things such as the ruins of kraals, and old fountains.

On the one side there is Kgoele and the other is Mathokwane, where my great-grandmother, Selloane, is buried. On the same road, you find Kurutlele on the left as you drive towards Bethlehem. That mountain too is flat on top. Ahead, is another flat mountain called Matikwane. That whole area, all the way to Bethlehem – all of it – was the land of Tshehlo.

In 1833, Piet Retief, the famous Boer Voortrekker, came through Aliwal North during the Great Trek. In Aliwal North there are rapids but they managed to cross the river and they headed to Winburg and then turned towards Senekal, Paul Roux and Bethlehem, all the way to Mautse.

When Piet Retief was between Senekal and Paul Roux, he was in the land of Tshehlo. He even wrote him a letter. Tshehlo reigned there although his father Nkejane was still alive. He had between ten and twelve wives and households (the number has not been agreed upon) and we, the family of Chapatso, are his children. To clarify: Chapatso was the grandson of Tshehlo, and his name is currently used as a surname by others in the Mofokeng family. What this means is that there are two family surnames: Mofokeng and Chapatso.

By the late 1800s, the Chapatsos were on the hill of Madraereng, where they lived together.

* * *

It is here that my grandfather Mongangane, the man who would eventually shake mountains, was born on 14 September 1914. That place is known as Riga. All the farms of this area are on Tshehlo's land.

The farms were registered in Winburg, but the Boers complained that Winburg was too far to travel, so the town of Senekal was established. It was named after Commandant General Frederik Senekal, who commanded the soldiers during the war to drive Basotho out of the Free State. He was killed by Basotho. The Boers say he ran out of bullets and the Basotho ran them over.

So this town of Senekal was established on the land of Tshehlo, at the foot of Kgoele, and blood was spilt here too in the many tussles that took place as Whites encroached and claimed for themselves land that already belonged to others.

There is a river called Thethana there. Mongangane told a story of how, when he converted his mother Selloane to the NG Kerk, he took her sangoma's tools and threw them in the river.

There is only one river that you cross when you climb the mountain and it's called Thethana. Piet Retief also crossed this river while heading to Natal, where he was later killed by the Zulu king Dingaan. He spent five days in the land of Tshehlo.

While there, Retief and his fellow travellers, over 2 000 men and women, walked along the river looking for flat areas. Thethana river provided him and his livestock of cows and horses with water.

Ellenberger counts BaMoojane separately from Bafokeng because of the large number they reached in the 1600s: some 2 000 people. When Retief encountered them in 1833, they were probably five times more.

The BaMoojane were known to be successful agriculturalists. They planted mealies, *mabele* (sorghum), sugar cane, beans, watermelon and pumpkin. Retief and his people sold some of their cows and sheep in exchange for the BaMoojane's fresh produce.

On a map of South Africa drawn by missionary Thomas Arbousset when he explored the Free State and passed by Lindley and Senekal, where Tshehlo lived, not a single mountain or river carried an Afrikaans or English name. He documented the landmarks in Sesotho as he was walking with Basotho.

In this map, BaMoojane shared the border with Bataung ba ha Moletsane, who owned the land between Winburg and Kroonstad. There were other people called Dihoja, who were north of us, and Batlokwa of Sekonyela at a distance.

Today we still have a letter written by Retief to the rulers of the area, including Tshehlo, Sekonyela and Moshoeshoe, explaining that his mission was to pass through as he was heading to Natal. He also wrote to Andries Stockenström, the deputy governor of the Cape Province based in Grahamstown, and it was published in the *Grahamstown Journal*.

They headed to Paul Roux after five days and at the NG Kerk building in Paul Roux there still stands a statue of a man and of carts and cows in remembrance of Retief's passage through the area.

Woefully, there is no such monument to remind us of Tshehlo.

Tshehlo's descendants have now scattered all over Lesotho and South Africa. Some are found in Botha-Bothe, Pitseng and Sebalabala in the district of Teyateyaneng in Lesotho. There are many more in Herschel in the Eastern Cape, and in eastern Free State towns such as Bethlehem and Lindley, and further afield in Welkom and Sasolburg in the northern parts of the Free State and the Vaal.

* * *

My grandfather lived in Riga on the Thethana river, and he went to school in Rosendal when he was 14 years of age. This was not unusual at that time as there was little formal education for Black children in the late 1920s. When he went to school he had already been initiated.

Mongangane told us that his father, Takatso, had sent him to school in Rosendal where he stayed with his aunt, Takatso's sister. The school my grandfather went to had been built with mud bricks. Later, the mud-brick structure was torn down and a new one was built. That too, was eventually torn down, and now there is a new school on the same premises where my grandfather was taught to read and write.

The school wasn't too far from where other family of Mongangane lived in Madraereng – probably about an hour's walk.

From Rosendal, Mongangane went to Libertas, before heading to Thaba Nchu to attend the Moroka Missionary Institution with his friend Fred Motsatse, a teacher's son.

He completed Standard 6 (today's Grade 8) there. His catechism certificate shows that he was confirmed as a member of the NG Kerk. To be clear, he was confirmed as a member of the main Dutch Reformed Church, the one that was later seen as the church for White people. He was not confirmed in the NG Kerk in Afrika, which is the church that was meant for Blacks.

That Mongangane was confirmed in this NG Kerk is an important detail from a family religious history perspective.

His father, Takatso, was an elder and preacher of the African Methodist Episcopal Church (AME Church), which had come to South Africa from the United States. Takatso couldn't read or write but was well versed in the Bible and he held church services every Sunday.

When the time came for Mongangane to attend catechism classes, there was no AME Church in Thaba Nchu. He travelled home to consult with his father. What was he to do?

Takatso understood his son's dilemma and encouraged him to attend any church closest to him.

That was how the NG Kerk was introduced into our family,

a decision that would have a great influence on our lives for generations.

Teacher Motsatse, who was Mongangane's friend Fred's father, was an elder of the NG Kerk. Mongangane joined them and charted a new course for us.

When it was time for his confirmation, Mongangane was told to find a Christian English name. He looked through the newspapers and spotted the name Wilfred and fell in love with it, and so he christened himself Wilfred.

It may seem strange to us today, but he never told his father that he was now Wilfred. His siblings, cousins and relatives didn't know who Wilfred was either; they knew him as Mongangane. It's probable that his future father-in-law, Ou Chaane, in Libertas knew the name because they were close and shared the Bible together.

* * *

The school he was at stopped at Standard 6 and so Mongangane had to move on. There was no high school in the Orange Free State – at least not for Africans. By this time, the Boers had taken the whole of the Free State and turned the land into farms. Then the republic became a British colony after the Boer War and subsequently a part of the Union of South Africa in 1910. Most schools for Black children were in Lesotho, started by French missionaries, and Thaba Nchu stood out as a Black principality. Basutoland, as it was known then, had become a British Crown Colony in 1884.

Under colonial rule, and as a direct result of the Land Act of 1913, which allocated a mere seven per cent of land to the majority while Whites were allowed to enjoy the other 93 per cent, Blacks were constantly being squeezed into smaller spaces with no facilities, and no prospect of development. This stifled the advancement of the African race, while Europeans had the convenience of physical and geographic space to develop their economic status as well as their culture.

Mongangane's father Takatso had worked in Port Elizabeth (now called Gqeberha) in the Eastern Cape, possibly at the harbour, which is where most of the work was for Basotho at the time. Many Basotho worked in the Cape, and Port Elizabeth was one of the most popular destinations. He worked there until he developed asthma and when he got back home to Madraereng, he couldn't work on the farm for the White man because of this chronic condition. The head of the family worked on the farm and his absence, due to old age or ill health, one of his sons had to take up his position. In his place, he elected Seabata, Mongangane's younger brother, to hold the contract with the Boer.

With all the money Takatso returned with, he managed to buy himself cattle and horses. One of his famous horses was called Moscow, a mare that bore several foals over the years. Takatso became one of the wealthiest men in Riga and boasted a horse-drawn cart.

Takatso must have seen the value of education when he was in Port Elizabeth among the amaXhosa. It made such an impact on him that when he returned, he said to Mongangane, 'You will not work for the White man, you will go to school.'

And so Takatso anointed Mongangane as the one who would break the chain of servitude that had shackled the Mofokeng family in the eastern Orange Free State.

Mongangane was the first one in the whole clan of Chapatso to go to school. The rest of his family, his elders and peers, the brothers and cousins throughout all the different family branches never went to school. Of his entire generation, he was the first and only one to go through the doors of education.

He was the chosen one.

3
Marabi in Magogogong

Even in a state of dereliction, Germiston Station on Railway Street stands out as an enduring landmark. The building is majestic and carries the old-world architectural charm of a crown palace. It is painted in decadent red, violet and cream, and its colonial design reminds passers-by of a long-gone era.

The hands of time are still on the four clocks on the sides of the dome on top of the building. I can imagine how, at the height of its operation, Germiston Station rivalled the likes of Grand Central in New York and King's Cross in London in terms of busyness. It is also the largest railway junction in South Africa with rail-repair shops populating its vicinity.

It bustles on a Friday afternoon. Music booms from stalls selling everything from Zulu *imbadada* (traditional shoes made out of tyres) to *mohodu* (tripe). The synthesiser-heavy Tsonga disco music and the call-and-response praise-poetry-laced Sesotho *mohobelo* take turns to fuel the energy as I make my way through the maze-like design of the station precinct. In the time of the Covid-19 pandemic, forget social distancing here. Hordes and hordes pour out of the corridors and corners of the station rushing to the nearby taxi rank. Trains might have stopped operating due to rampant vandalism and theft of infrastructure, but this is still a transport node.

I wonder whether some of the peak-hour pedestrian traffic numbers have hastened their steps to get to the Cheeky Tiger bar at the corner. A quick one-for-the-road. The logo of the establishment bears a tiger baring its teeth and two strippers on poles. I didn't go in to check the action behind the darkened windows.

Everybody walks fast in this neighbourhood. As if it's a race for their lives.

I try to get to the office section of the station but a polite woman tells me to not bother. With the train service suspended indefinitely, the place is a ghost town and security personnel will not allow me to wander about.

I follow groups of men ascending a steep flight of steps. Heaven knows where they are going but I will see when I get there. At the top of the steps I find myself at a vantage point, and I am able to take in the extent of this station. I count over a dozen rails converging and diverging on multiple platforms below. Trains from all directions carrying passengers and goods once made a stop here.

So while the sound of trains is no longer part of the ambience here, the remnants are there to show that in the 1930s this was a destination of choice as many young Black men trekked from their towns, villages and farms hoping to strike it rich amid the industrial boom of Germiston.

The irony is overwhelming that this station – so central to building Johannesburg and the surrounding metros – has sunk into disrepair. The effects can be felt in the economy and productivity of a city. It is heartbreaking that this station serviced the needs of the White bosses as it provided a port for labour supply, yet this same infrastructure fails to serve the poor Black labourers who cannot travel to work economically, reliably and efficiently without the rail service. What was once a symbol of Black exploitation, later became the saving grace of the Black labour in need of affordable transportation to ferry them from their distant locations to the industrial zone. But now the affordable transportation is no more due to neglect and corruption.

Poor people are undone here and there is no outrage.

And it was under a Black government's watch that decrepitude set in.

* * *

I find myself at Germiston Station because this is an important geographical bookmark in the story of the life of my grandfather, Mongangane Mofokeng. This is where he would have arrived from Thaba Nchu in 1936, having completed his Standard 6, the highest class at the Moroka Missionary Institution.

So what would Mongangane do with all this education that his father believed would protect him?

He didn't stay long at Madraereng after completing Standard 6. It was just a farm that could offer no stimulation for a man of his education and sophistication, not to mention dreams and ambitions. His older cousin, Ephraim, was living it up Marabi-style in the rapidly industrialising Germiston and had promised to show the young, educated Mongangane a good time in the bright city lights. Mongangane bade his family farewell, hopped on a train and was welcomed by Ephraim at the Germiston Station.

The culture of Marabi, fuelled by the music, was in full swing with the raucous lilting melodies and catchy rhythms hanging in the air. It was improvisational and original.

In the cities and towns, habits and opportunities changed. Women brewed and sold liquor, and shebeen parties became the culture of the slum yards. The drinking often resulted in casual sex and broken family relationships. So pervasive was Marabi that the *Bantu World* newspaper noted in April 1932 that the 'new' music had turned many parts of the Reef into a perfect pandemonium.

Mongangane Mofokeng, left, strikes a pose in a Johannesburg studio with a friend known only as Motsamai. This is the oldest picture of Mongangane in existence. It was taken when he was in his 20s, in the mid-1930s. PHOTO: FAMILY ALBUM

For my grandfather, plucked out of sleepy Thaba Nchu, Germiston pulsated to a different rhythm. It was overwhelming for him to see the crowds competing for space. Ephraim provided a steady hand in the maelstrom of a city booming with unprecedented industrialisation. From all directions – KwaZulu in the east, Sekhukhuneland in the north, Basutoland (now Lesotho) in the south and Xhosaland in the deep south – the trains churned them out on the platforms so that they could pursue their dreams for a better life.

The words of 'Stimela', the song by jazz giant Hugh Masekela that he recorded in 1974, come to mind. The song was a battle cry against the unjust migrant labour system, and he framed the lyrics with the image of the coal train that carried many young Black men into South African towns so that they could earn wages by selling their labour at a very low cost.

The song delivers a poignant reminder of the living conditions of these African miners, and labourers, who stayed in hostels in unhygienic filth. He could just as well have meant the shanty slums like Magogogong where Mongangane lived.

While the train took the men closer to the big city where they could earn money, it was also an object of disdain because it took them away from home and delivered them into danger.

Masekela sang that these men in the city 'cursed' the coal train that had brought them to Johannesburg.

* * *

Magogogong, which literally meant 'a place of shacks', was Mongangane's base as he found his bearings in the city. It fell under the town of Alberton but was close enough to Germiston – it took a single train ride of a few minutes to get there. It was located near the now defunct Newmarket Racecourse and was later demolished by the authorities. It was a typical 1930s slum: overcrowded, noisy, smelly, violent and bustling. Brick houses interspersed with shacks created the patchwork pattern of the settlement.

The time of Marabi and the Black community's migration to cities is often romanticised. But this was a difficult period for Black people. Life was hard and it was perilous. People were packed on top of one other amid the inhospitable conditions in the barracks, hostels and slums, as Masekela painted so vividly in 'Stimela'.

The scramble for resources became a daily tussle that bred criminality. The squalor was awful. Dead mice, cats and dogs rotted in the streets. Sometimes there would be human bodies, victims of crimes in the night. There were no services. The conditions were toxic. But with the money economy driving young Black men from their homes in villages and small towns across South Africa to the Reef, places like Magogogong were never in short supply of new starry-eyed 'Jims come to Joburg', emerging from the pond of naivety. And these men were often the targets and the happy hunting ground of *clevas* (tsotsis), pickpockets and charlatans.

Mongangane had a softer landing pad than most as he had the support structure of his older cousins Ephraim and Naha, who joined them later. In African tradition, first cousins are regarded as brothers and sisters if their fathers are siblings, as was the case with the trio.

The story goes that when the two brothers, Mongangane and Naha went to register at Home Affairs in Alberton, they opted to dump the surname Chapatso and chose Mofokeng, which was their clan name. But Mongangane told a different version of this story later in life. He explained that the original family surname was Mofokeng and that Chapatso was one of their ancestors, and so they were correcting the family lineage.

Ephraim stayed a Chapatso and went on to become a legend of Thokoza township when Magogogong was demolished, and the people were forcibly moved to the new location. In fact, there is a Chapatso street in Thokoza named after him.

Although he hadn't trained to become an evangelist, he was well known at Natalspruit Hospital for his prayer sessions. He went from ward to ward praying for the sickly. Those who heard him say he was poetic and rousing.

I sometimes wonder whether it was his example that planted the seed of going into the ministry in Mongangane. Interestingly, Naha went on to become an atheist and often protested about Christian rites and prayer at family gatherings.

* * *

It would not take Mongangane long before he secured a job at a bakery on the busy President Street in Germiston. Here, he learned how to make bread and he did kitchen duty. With the money he made, he could support his mother back home at Madraereng. His father having recently passed away, the responsibility of ensuring that the family was looked after fell on his shoulders as the eldest son.

Living in the epicentre of the Germiston mining and industry boom, Mongangane quickly learned to be wise, to outsmart the tsotsis from Benoni who liked to trick the Jims come to Joburg (or Germiston) from rural Orange Free State, Natal, and Northern and Southern Transvaal, as the provinces were known then.

He had to shake off the image of a Thaba Nchu *bari* (a country bumpkin) and walk the talk of the streets of Germiston. And so a wardrobe change was called for. He stepped out in a three-piece suit topped with a hat and, *voila*, he could walk down President Street without sticking out like a countryman. Under the hat, his short hair was parted in the middle as the cool style of the time dictated.

Thrust into the middle of a booming city with different cultures converging to create a melting pot, it must have been here that he developed his lifelong love for fish and chips. It had become a city staple brought over by the British entrepreneurs and it became what distinguished gentlemen ate.

I suspect it was during this initiation time that he also developed his skills in front of the camera. As a rule, Mongangane never looked directly at the camera. Well, except for the image at the start of this chapter. He insisted on looking away and fixing his eyes on an object nearby or far away. He considered it, he said in later years, crass to smile and make eye contact with the camera.

He did a lot of adjusting in his new landscape. Coming from an agrarian economy, where open tracts of land were cultivated for mealies, sunflower and sorghum, he found the smoke-filled skies of Germiston a surprise. If it wasn't the choo-choo train that had brought him to the city, then it was the steel factories that seemed to spew smoke all day and night as they melted metal. The sound of machinery and tools – of drilling and hammering, scraping and cutting, the shouting and banging and hissing and general bedlam – of a growing, thriving early nineteenth century colonial city had replaced the serenity of crops growing to fullness in the pristine air of the Orange Free State.

Mongangane was soon to learn his place with the Black Jacks, the police who monitored the carrying of the dreaded dompas, an identity document Black men had to carry with them at all times. He may have learned his way around the city, but he could not outsmart or outrun the damned police that stopped Black men at a whim. As historian Jacob Dlamini posited, the South African police put together civil, judicial, military and political administration under one umbrella, and this explained why the colonial and apartheid police acquired a reputation for brutality as they protected White power. The dompas – a domestic passport system meant to manage urbanisation and migrant labour – was the devastatingly simple tool for enforcing this regime on the average Black person trying to make their way in the urbanising landscape of early apartheid.

A turning point for the educated young man from Thaba Nchu, who liked to read the newspapers and the Bible and to eat fish and chips, was when he was arrested for the first time. By his account, it was an experience that left him shaken. While rushing to work from Magogogong one morning, he was stopped by police and that was when he realised that he had forgotten the all-important green document. It meant a few days in the police holding cells.

The incident made him think twice about his move to the big smoke and having to grapple daily with this kind of oppressive restriction on how and where Black people were allowed to move around a city that was being built by the sweat of their own brows. It was his determination and willpower that kept him sane for the time he spent behind bars, usually about two to three days. He remembered how coming to Germiston meant better opportunities for him and that going back to Madraereng was not an option. He realised that the White man dominated and owned the streets, and the White man was unforgiving. Mongangane was to stay out of his way and to carry the dompas.

He left the cells a different man. The naivety was shattered and in its place was the grim reality of how severe segregation really was. So he marched on. While he made every effort to remember to carry the dompas, there were times it would disappear, or he would forget it and inevitably a Black Jack would tap him on his shoulder and that led to a night in the dark. He toughened up and simply followed the drill. It also helped that the employers knew the harsh reality their Black staff experienced and so he never lost his job at the bakery when he didn't pitch.

* * *

By the 1930s, the locations of the East Rand (now Ekurhuleni) had become ethnically mixed and also housed a growing population of African women. The hybridity, self-assertion, self-confidence and self-construction stamped itself indelibly on the cultures of these freewheeling locations.

Add to this heady mix a booming economy in the form of gold mining and you have a rush of opportunity-seekers from all over the country. The historians put the number of Africans in the East Rand at about 5 000 in 1890 and 22 years later, in 1912, it stood at 69 127. Germiston, which was founded in 1886 and became a self-governing municipality in 1903, immediately took steps to control the haphazard mushrooming of African settlements around the mining areas.

To accommodate the influx, a negligible number of municipal houses for Blacks were built. The typical pattern across the East Rand towns was to trim costs by providing serviced plots or stands, upon which stand holders could erect wood-and-iron structures, sometimes aided by loans or low-cost building materials furnished by municipal authorities. This mostly self-built environment opened up a number of spaces and opportunities that allowed its residents to escape some of the structures of urban control and which served to soften the harsh regimen of Black urban life.

The new Black work-seekers who thronged Germiston found accommodation as sub-tenants on the stands rented from the municipality by existing tenants in places like Magogogong. It wasn't until 1950 that the sub-tenants moved to the newly built township of Natalspruit (now Katlehong) following the relentless agitation campaign of trade unionist Raphael Phalime of the South African Clothing Workers Union and his friend Johannes Madieleng.

In the 1930s, the impact of the Great Depression in the United States of America reverberated around the world and declining economic effects pinched South Africa. They hit agriculture hardest and the country abandoned the Gold Standard and delinked its currency from a fixed quantity of gold, sending the price of the metal to double.

The boom gave rise to the secondary industrial development that exploded from 1935 and the biggest beneficiaries were Germiston and Benoni where factories mushroomed. After World War II, more factories – such as South African General Electric, Oxygen and Thermal Welding Products, and Robert Hudson and Sons – went up in Germiston.

Elsewhere in the East Rand airports were going up. First was Rand Airport in Germiston, then Palmietfontein in the south of the town, and then Jan Smuts in Kempton Park. As a result of these multiple transformations, Ekurhuleni's growth rate between 1921 and 1960 exceeded that of Johannesburg. By the end of the 1940s, Ekurhuleni employed one-third of the industrial employees of the Witwatersrand.

Mongangane joined the employment queue at Rand Airport and secured a job as a security guard, which paid a little more than the bakery on President Street. At one point this was the busiest airport in Africa and in the southern hemisphere.

The arrests and harassment by the Black Jacks continued unabated and not even a security guard was exempted from carrying a dompas. But the skin had hardened and the lashes from the baton were expected, along with the pushing and shoving.

Still, something was not sitting right with my grandfather. How can a human being be treated in this way? This was no different to the sheep at Madraereng. Not to mention the state of housing for Africans: smelly waters breeding mosquitoes, dead cats, smoke from the hundreds of small shacks huddled together. Surely none of these factors alone could ever bring any wellness. It was a helpless and desolate place to be in.

4
Coming of age

Evangelist Jerry Mofokeng – not to be confused with the well-known actor – is the first son of Mongangane. He is my father's eldest brother, and my eldest paternal uncle. My father was the last born.

Jerry is now an octogenarian with the proverbial spring in his step even though his gait has slowed down. He is of slight build and wears a shy smile. His soft-spoken and gentle nature belies his spirited pulpit persona. He transforms into a roaring preacher. His voice goes up a few decibels and he becomes extremely animated.

I met him at his house in Thokoza and our conversation allowed me insight I'd not had before on the dynamics of the Mofokeng family. I went to see him in search of answers. Jerry has always been present in our lives. He never stops regaling me with stories of eventful travels with my mother – his sister-in-law – in some old Peugeot on the way to rural Gelukspan to visit my grandparents. The two of them lived and worked in Johannesburg and so would take the four-hour journey together through Carletonville, Ventersdorp and Coligny to Lichtenburg. There were no mobile phones in those days, so it became tradition that when they reached Lichtenburg, they would stop and call the landline at home from the last tickey box – which is what coin-operated public phones were called – to share the news that they were safe and announce that they would soon be home in Gelukspan.

As the eldest son, Jerry had always been independent of the family. His mother's name was Mahadi Chaane, and he grew up in Libertas with her family. From there, he moved to Kroonstad with his aunt, Masabata, before going to school in Makapanstad, in present-day North West. When he was finished with school, he moved to Welkom to work as a painter and went to the seminary his father attended. The Stofberg Seminary by then had moved from Viljoensdrif near Vereeniging in the northern Orange Free State to Qwaqwa, due to the Group Areas Act.

Jerry started his evangelist career in Thokoza and then moved to Katlehong where he had a ministry for over three decades. He moved back to Thokoza to live as a pensioner. He had never really lived at home with his siblings and parents, seeing them only during holidays.

I asked him to take me back to Libertas, a place named after the ancient Roman personification of liberty. Libertas hardly represented liberty for the Black farm workers there. It's little wonder that the Basotho corrupted it to the meaningless Lebertasi, because liberty was meaningless to them.

A recent trip I had taken to Libertas had yielded no real clues for me in my family story. There had been a tree or two, and ruins that were believed to have been a stable for horses. There are no houses to tell stories, only foundations leave a trace of what was once there. But Jerry had walked these streets, and I wanted to know what they had been like.

He remembered the busy train station near the village and Libertas Primary School where both he and his mother before him had been educated.

In between schooling, Mahadi and her sisters worked on the farm along with their mother, Nkileng Rose Dlamini, doing kitchen duty, cleaning and ironing. It was one of the conditions that the daughters work in the *huis* (White boss's house) in shifts.

Jerry's maternal grandfather, Ou (old man) Mmuso Chaane

worked for the White farm owner Flip Heyns looking after animals and cultivating the fields. Jerry and the other youngsters in the village, including his younger brother Bernard who joined him later, and their cousin Tshokolo (their mothers were sisters), also worked in the fields in winter when extra pairs of hands were needed to harvest mealies.

The Chaane household was a compound of clay houses and huts decorated in *ditema*, the traditional Sotho mural designs. Some of these structures had roofs of iron sheeting and the others were thatched, especially *mekgoro* (kitchens). The family lived on a healthy diet of vegetables, chickens and eggs. Ou Chaane owned livestock, including cows and sheep. He was a wealthy man with a stable full of horses. If ever you doubted a man's wealth, you had to look at the frame of his cart. His was made out of steel and decorated with wood. It dazzled from a routine new lick of paint – just the affirmation you needed that he was well off.

The horses were well fed, glistened in daylight from all the care Mahadi and her elder sister Mamokgasi and younger sister Makanono showered on them. The youngest, Masabata was still too small to be running after horses and the younger boys too busy. Moifadi had expressed his interest to be in the army while Thabiso was seldom home.

Jerry remembered how Ou Chaane always slaughtered a cow in winter so that he could keep the family and grandchildren well fed.

This ancestral place is not too far from the towns of Paul Roux and Senekal. Mongangane had become a friend of the Chaane family. As the most educated young man in the area, he regularly visited the Chaanes to read the Bible to Ou Chaane who, though illiterate, possessed a Bible, and was a preacher of the Apostolic Faith Mission Church. His eldest daughters could read, but he preferred it when Mongangane did.

* * *

Back in Johannesburg, a new steel factory had set up shop in the city centre on Jeppe Street and manual labour was in demand. After years in the shelter of his brother-cousins Ephraim and Naha, and the unwelcome intrusions by the police, Mongangane had been confident to strike it out on his own. He rushed to Jeppe Street where he was signed up as a casual labourer at the steel factory. When he visited home with the news of his new job, his younger cousins were quite tickled by the unusual sound of 'Jeppe' Street. They sniggered and nicknamed him 'Jepita' and the moniker stuck for a while. When the factory moved to Sauer Street, it didn't translate into a new pet name.

Having moved from Magogogong, Mongangane set up camp roughly ten kilometres away in George Goch, which, while still in the east, as Germiston was, was closer to the city of Johannesburg. George Goch was named after the mayor of Johannesburg from 1904 to 1905.

Here, Mongangane immersed himself in the culture of the place. The weekend tradition of soccer matches became his favourite pastime. Not that he was any good as a soccer player, but he could dribble his way past most opponents. The weekdays were tough and heavy on the body and the soul, but the weekends on the soccer pitch replenished what was lost in the fire of the steel company.

As a young man in his early 20s, Mongangane also got to experience Sophiatown, its magic and its broken dreams. But its 'roughness' put him off and he never stayed in the area. When he next moved, it was westwards, where he settled in Fietas, which is present-day Mayfair, and places like Newclare used to be his stomping ground.

Writer Miriam Tlali shared a glimpse of the ruthlessness of that time, but also celebrated the vibrancy of life in the face of adversity. She wrote of the 1930s: 'We used to call Newclare "Sdikidiki" then. There, life was really life. The streets were always full of people, young and old. Beggars, robbers, pickpockets, drunkards, prostitutes, prayer women, ministers – everything. But everybody was happy.'

By the time Mongangane was 25, he'd scraped together enough savings from all his work to finally afford lobola, the bride price (known as 'mahadi' in Sesotho) for the beautiful and feisty Mahadi he'd been eyeing during his visits to read the Bible to Ou Chaane.

With Mahadi pregnant with their first child, Mongangane went home to finalise their nuptials and, in October 1939, at a sweet traditional and western wedding at the Chaanes' in Libertas, Mongangane and Mahadi got married. Following Sesotho tradition, Mahadi was welcomed to the Bafokeng with a new name, and she was to be known as MaThabo. This, Basotho would say, is so that their first-born son would carry that name. The following month, their son was born.

He was named Thabo Makuoe Jerry. Makuoe was the name of one of Mongangane's paternal uncles. Later in life he would be popularly known as Jerry.

* * *

Mongangane entered the 1940s as a family man. He had proven his independence and resilience as a city man. Now he had a wife and a small baby back home in the Free State to provide for.

Things were not that easy for Mahadi though. Life as a new bride in the Mofokeng household proved to be hard on her.

Mongangane's younger sister, Mapiletsa, was possessive of her brother who worked in the big city, and she became controlling of whatever he brought home, from groceries to kitchen utensils.

She made Mahadi's time as a young *ngwetsi* (daughter-in-law) unbearable, teasing and mocking her, and forbidding her to use the things her brother purchased. 'Don't touch it! My brother bought it! I will use it as I like,' is how Mahadi once explained that Mapiletsa would taunt her. Things got so out of hand that she eventually bundled up her baby Jerry and ran away back home to Libertas.

It would take Mongangane a trip back home to diffuse the situation. He resolved that Mahadi would not return to Madraereng. Instead she would join him in Johannesburg where he had found a new home in a township in Roodepoort. The factory had trekked westward from Sauer Street to Roodepoort and Mongangane had sought lodgings in the West Rand.

After a lengthy wait, the family eventually settled in the Shelters Number 2 section of the new township of Orlando that was fast developing into what would become known as Soweto.

Jerry, meanwhile, was left in the care of the Chaanes, with Masabata, Mahadi's youngest sister, watching over him.

* * *

Jerry's contribution to filling out the story of my paternal grandparents was enormously helpful to me.

5
1625 Shelters Number 2, Orlando

Jerry was Mongangane and Mahadi's first born. Next came Takatso, the second of five boys, who was named for Mongangane's father. I am the son of their youngest son Moses.

I make a nervous trip to rural Devon to see my second uncle. The small you-blink-you-miss-it town is wedged in the farming valleys on the border of Mpumalanga and Gauteng. I am nervous because my GPS navigation cannot take me to Palmietdrift farm. Instead, I have to rely on my cousin Mpho's directions.

'Right at the curve. Just before the big tree, turn right again and the dirt road will lead you to a small village,' he told me. I had to remember these words, in that order, all the way for some 50 kilometres as I made my way to Devon. I couldn't afford to miss the spot, so I drove unblinkingly for the two or three kilometres after the highway offramp lest I end up in the beyond-of-the-beyonds of rural Mpumalanga.

My efforts were rewarded when the dirt road emerged to my right, just before the large blue gum tree to my left. It was a bumpy ride. The road hadn't been graded for a while and was potholed. Wild grass grew in clumps.

My uncle doesn't live in the windswept village on my right, but in the *ou huis* (old house) perched up on the little hill.

Takatso Mofokeng is Mpho's father. He was named after his paternal grandfather. He is the child that lived with Mongangane and Mahadi the longest, travelling with them from place to place.

He is now a retired university professor of theology and a keen historian. In his quiet years running his farm, he has dedicated time to documenting, collecting and preserving what's left and known of the family history.

His travels have taken him through most of the Free State towns and through the capital city of Bloemfontein. He has also been to Lesotho, travelling up and down the towns and villages as he dug out the forgotten history of Bafokeng as well as the church that he helped birth, the Uniting Reformed Church in Southern Africa (URCSA).

The URCSA is a mutation of the NG Kerk in Afrika, which is not to be confused with the NG Kerk. The former is a 'daughter' church; the latter is the mother church. The NG Kerk in Afrika was formed to cater for African believers. It was for Blacks. The mother church was for Whites. The NG Kerk in Afrika was called Kereke ya Fora by Basotho and Batswana. This anomaly – calling the Dutch church 'Church of the French', is something I investigate in later chapters.

The fundamental racism at the heart of the church's structure is something Takatso and his peers tackled when forming the URCSA.

Takatso was one of the instrumental figures in 1994 that gathered in Belhar, Cape Town to finalise the talks between the unification of the NG Kerk in Afrika for Blacks and the NG Kerk Sending for the Coloureds. The project is still incomplete until the Whites and the Indians meet at the pulpit of non-racialism, hence the name 'Uniting' – and not 'United'.

He welcomes me into his spacious farmhouse on a chilly Saturday morning. We settle in what looks like his office with files neatly stacked in rows. It is close to the kitchen where he makes us a cuppa before we start our talk about his experiences and life with his parents.

Professor Takatso Mofokeng at his farmhouse in Devon. PHOTO: AUTHOR

'I was born in 1942,' Takatso began. 'I can't say exactly where, but my baptismal certificate says I was baptised at the NG Kerk in Steynsrus in the Free State, but officially I will say I was born in Orlando and went to Orlando Primary School in Orlando East, just across the railway line in Mlamlankunzi.

'Ntate (Father) knew Nelson Mandela as a young lawyer and activist, along with Oliver Tambo in town. I also knew James Sofasonke Mpanza. At that time, people were politicised. They had to be politicised. They knew White people as oppressors. Ntate told me that they were oppressors. I can't recall how many times he got arrested over dompas and vagrancy.

'He had a green dompas that he carried with him, and he would return home to tell us how, while they were playing soccer and left their clothes by pitch side, police suddenly appeared and bundled them into vans for not having their dompasse on them – while playing soccer. All the police would say was that they could explain themselves at the police station. He would only be released after we took his pass to the station.'

Takatso could not recall how they ended up at Orlando Shelters. They had lived in a small township in nearby Roodepoort before moving to the Shelters.

He described the house at the Shelters as a one-room structure made out of cheap bricks, similar to today's RDP houses, the houses built by the government for low-income families. The room, or house, had a small window. The Mofokeng household comprised his parents, Takatso and his younger brother Motswantweng Ephraim, who was born in 1944 and was popularly known as Spanky. Jerry remained in the Free State with the Chaanes. While the parents occupied the bedroom, the two boys slept in the kitchen, an extension of the home made out of corrugated iron sheets. Due to the small size of the houses, families used to add rooms using iron sheets to create more space.

It was in that house that the Mofokengs welcomed their fourth son, Bernard, who was born in the Shelters in 1947.

* * *

The streets of Orlando Shelters were narrow, and the houses were lined up in rows, back to back. Holes were dug in the small spaces between the houses to hide traditional beer from the authorities. This illicit business put bread on the table for shebeen queens and other women and men trying to make ends meet. That practice of digging holes gave rise to the name *seepamokoti* (a hole digger), a job reserved for the lowest rung of labourers or failures at life, who were paid in alcohol, never cash.

My grandmother with my Uncle Bernard, who was popularly
known as Benny, in Orlando in the mid-1940s. PHOTO: FAMILY ALBUM

Takatso reminded me of *Khawuleza*, the 1950s hit song originally recorded by Dorothy Masuka and made popular by Miriam Makeba when she released it in 1966. There's a line where a young girl pleads with her mother to hurry up and hide the beer to avoid being arrested by the authorities.

Takatso said this song referred to the practice when the Black Jack municipal police would come to raid houses. They came with canes to prod the earth and where it sounded hollow, they would dig out the alcohol and dispose of it, if not arrest the brewers.

Takatso started school in Orlando and played in the streets with Spanky and other children. Their neighbours were amaXhosa and they gave Motswantweng the nickname of Spanky, probably to save themselves from biting their tongues from the threatening Sotho name that meant 'the one who returned from the war'. The Mofokeng children picked up the isiXhosa language from these children as they spent a lot of time together.

* * *

Mongangane woke up at the crack of dawn and rode a train to Roodepoort for work. He returned home late when his sons were already sleeping. They caught hazy glances of him in mid-slumber on some days.

'As a result, Spanky and I didn't have a good memory of our father,' Takatso shared. 'We didn't have a lively relationship with him because he was simply not there during the week. The only time we saw him and we could relate to him was during the weekend. Some Saturdays we would visit our aunt Makanono, my mother's younger sister, in Springs where she worked as a domestic worker. The trip by train to the East Rand was a family outing we relished.

'On Sundays, without fail, we went to the NG Kerk in Roodepoort for church held in a shack and Ntate was very active. There was a very lively community at the church, under Evangelist Santho whom I recall well. I didn't even know that there was a White minister, I only heard that from Ntate later in life.'

Mongangane had been introduced to the NG Kerk in Thaba Nchu where he lived with the Motsatse family while studying. His father was an elder in the African Methodist Episcopal Church (AME Church), but the Motsatses belonged to the NG Kerk and there was no AME nearby. He attended the catechism class and was confirmed. He never reunited with the AME Church, instead giving his life to the Dutch Reformed Church.

What Takatso remembered about his mother, Mahadi, was that she had always been enterprising. She traded in many things, perfecting the art and science of buying and selling. Alcohol, it would seem, was never one of her trade items.

She targeted Mongangane's fellow employees at the factory in Roodepoort. Every evening, Mahadi smothered bread she'd sliced in butter and jam before wrapping the sandwiches in foil and stacking them neatly in a small tin suitcase Mongangane took to work every morning where he sold them to colleagues. As a housewife, Mahadi found a way to contribute to the family kitty using her entrepreneurial instincts and her industriousness.

Mongangane was not that inclined towards business, especially after one incident that put him off such ventures. He opened a shop with a friend and business partner, who ran the operation while Mongangane worked in Roodepoort. It wasn't long before they were woken up in the night with the news that there had been a robbery at the store in the dark of the night and that it had been cleaned out.

'We rushed out to see what happened and found mealie meal poured all over the floor and the entire stock taken. That was the last time Ntate went into business, and he swore away from such dealings. We later learned that there was a suspicion that the partner might have been behind the burglary,' Takatso reminisced.

'On the other hand, Mme (Mother) remained in business for the rest of her life. Moses is the one who inherited that tradition of buying and selling.'

Moses was the last-born son, and he was my father.

* * *

Life in Orlando Shelters was, in fact, very sheltered. The architects of apartheid had won the battle of keeping the races apart and ensuring that the natives stayed where they'd been put.

'We didn't know White people while growing up,' said Takatso. 'I must have been five or six years old when I first saw a White person. It was a White boy and a White girl who came to Orlando Shelters Number 2 one weekend, probably a Sunday, because we were never around on Saturdays as we were playing soccer. The two came with a guitar and they sang for us, the other White person we saw was the security guard in the train to Springs.'

For Mongangane, two things mattered the most: church and football. More specifically, Orlando Pirates. The football team had become the pride and identity of the community and as a man from Orlando, he had little choice. He went to watch them in action wherever they played.

6
Once a Pirate, always a Pirate

I remember Mongangane in his 90s, hard of hearing and pressing his ear against his battery-powered transistor radio, as the announcer shrilled and grunted during a thrilling Soweto derby in which Orlando Pirates tackled arch-rivals Kaizer Chiefs. That image of my grandfather will stay with me forever.

His eyesight was failing him. Going to the stadium or watching soccer on TV was a futile exercise, so the wireless became his ally. It connected him to his past and probably reignited the fire and magic of a Pirates soccer match at Wemmer or Bantu Sports of the 1940s.

Orlando Pirates, currently a Premier Soccer League outfit in South Africa, carries so much rich history and heritage. According to information on the team's website, football was used as a political cover in the 1940s because during apartheid, the Black majority was not allowed to hold public gatherings in case these opportunities were used for political discussions.

Both church and soccer provided the cover for Blacks to get together, and the game gave the oppressed an opportunity to occasionally leave the country and escape the harsh living conditions if only for a few hours or days.

'The People's Club' was the subject of a 1991 dissertation by Richard Maguire that gave context and significance to the soccer team as a social institution that made an impact on the day-to-day lives of Black South Africans. Maguire said Orlando Pirates was an expression of urban African culture and that it generated passionate support both as a unifying force and a source of bitter division at the same time. The team became a symbol and the second family name of residents of Soweto as it entrenched itself deeper in the community.

Orlando Pirates started off as Orlando Boys Club FC in 1937 when soccer was a popular pastime in Black townships and school soccer was fertile turf for competition. The pitches were uneven, hard and sandy, and the players were barefoot and played in their school uniforms.

In 1938, they finished the season in a minor division of the Johannesburg Bantu Football Association (JBFA). Travelling on bicycles in fours or cutting across on foot to Sophiatown, they played at the Waterval grounds – barefoot and without a proper playing strip. Instead, they played in a variety of uncoordinated shirts. It was only when their first patron, Bethuel Mokgosinyana, a self-styled social worker, as some referred to him, took an interest in them in 1940 that they could play in a unifying kit.

Another influential figure behind the team was boxer Andries 'Pele Pele' Mkwanazi. Pirates was birthed in his house, two blocks away from the Boys Club. With a new and fearsome name, the jersey-less team took on competition on the football field and made rapid progress.

They were already competing in the Saturday League Division Two of the JBFA and were promoted to the Saturday League Division One in 1939. Their matches were usually played in the township or the city, either in Newclare or at the Wemmer Grounds, the headquarters of the JBFA.

They competed against teams from townships and ghettoes around Johannesburg as well as city-based sides of domestic servants or company employees. There were also Eastern Leopards, dominated by teachers and students from Kilnerton College based in George Goch (Eastern Native Township), and local rivals, Eastern Brothers.

Pirates also had the support of James Sofasonke Mpanza, the titanic leader of the squatter movement in Orlando and the man regarded as the father of the township. Mongangane told tales of how he was in the stands when Mpanza galloped on to the field on horseback ahead of the start of a much anticipated soccer clash. His eyes would light up and he would chuckle as he reminisced about those days. Soccer restored something in him and gave him control of his happiness. At a time when the oppressive world attacked the fabric of family and community, sport would stitch back what was taken away.

Elsewhere in Soweto, Swallows was patronised by Ntoyi, the leader of the Basotho formation calling themselves Russians. He organised a squatter camp in Moroka. African Morning Stars, in Sophiatown, was backed by big-time gangsters.

Interestingly, out of the three, Pirates is the only team that has an unbroken record of playing in the top flight league over 80 years later. Swallows returned to the PSL in the 2020/21 season under a different guise after five years in the lower leagues. They bought the status of another team that earned a promotion for the new season.

Written in the constitution of the club was that only boys from Orlando, or the children of Orlando residents, could play for Pirates and this made it the treasure of the community. The team would become an institution and a source of civic pride. Many clubs in other South African townships were called 'peoples' clubs' in their founding stages and rootedness, but none developed to the extent that Pirates did.

* * *

While the sense of community was deepened, for men, like Mongangane and his young sons, team sport provided a sustained close-knit group in the context of unprecedented urban upheaval, Maguire wrote in his thesis. Belonging in a team meant having friends, sharing a sense of loyalty and facing the struggle together, as well as pride in representing your block in the township.

Soccer was an agent of integration for migrants. In the early decades of organised football on the Witwatersrand, migrants from a particular area would form a club among themselves drawing membership from a wide range of occupations and even from different townships. For instance, Imperial Air Force was strictly for Basotho, and GPO Sweepers was for the labourers from Natal. In December, these township or city teams would return home, and play against their local brethren, spreading the popularity of the game.

Weekends of non-stop football action at Wemmer and Bantu Sports was an indulgence for diehard fans and casual spectators who lived in townships, hostels and slums. For a few hours, the monotony of shifts in factories and mines and the endless trouble of dompas checks were replaced by fervent jubilation and camaraderie. As Maguire put it, football was a means of maximising the quality of their lives. They ran tirelessly up and down the touchline as they exhorted their sides to greater efforts as if their lives depended on it, singing rousing isiZulu songs or stealing away from the action to take an illicit swig of home brew: whatever they did at the match, they took the opportunity to do what pleased them.

But these times were not simply an escape from the daily grind as the boot of apartheid was crushing the lives of countless Black South Africans. It was precious solace and succour for the soul. For my grandfather, whose thoughts were turning to a life outside of the pressures of the big city, it was a glimpse that there was perhaps another road opening up to him.

7

The making of an evangelist

At the NG Kerk in Roodepoort that congregated in a shack, Mongangane threw his life into the service of the church. He was a member of the MBB (Mokgatlo wa Badumedi ba Bakreste youth ministry) and upon seeing his leadership qualities, devotion and diligence, the senior pastors promoted him to elder. The fact that he had a natural talent for preaching and that his knowledge of the Bible was vast, also helped. Experience – dating back to the days when as a young man he read the scriptures to Ou Chaane, Mahadi's father – stood him in good stead.

Joining the seminary became the most natural step when the White minister offered him an opportunity to train as an evangelist. The evangelist's primary role was to be a missionary. His main task was to do field work recruiting converts, taking the word to the people and doing most of the convincing. The evangelist would also do pastoral care through *huisbesoek* (home visits), delivering sermons during church services, funerals and other events, as well as assisting with the administration of the church and effectively serving as the deputy to the minister under whose supervision he worked.

Back then, evangelists couldn't baptise or serve the holy communion. Strangely though, they were allowed to prepare the holy bread and wine. They just did not have the powers to deliver it to the members of the church.

Faced with the long hours in the steel factory, the unforgiving dompas Black Jacks and limited opportunities in the big city, heading to the seminary made sense to Mongangane. It would be a great place for him to further his studies and receive a qualification beyond the Standard 6 certificate he had received in Thaba Nchu.

Also, chances of improving the family's fortunes looked promising.

He already loved the gospel and was committed to the church in Roodepoort. The opportunity that had now been offered was a venture worth pursuing.

Mongangane and another young leader, Kgobokoe, along with their families, were sent off to Stofberg Gedenkskool in Viljoensdrif in the Orange Free State.

At this point, in 1949, the Mofokeng family had been allocated a house in the new township of Mofolo where they had planned to resettle in a bigger home than in the Shelters. But the decision was made to leave Orlando and Johannesburg and walk away from the new abode. Whatever became of the house is unclear, but Takatso seemed to remember his mother saying that Mongangane passed on the keys to a cousin of his known as Lebona, in his typical giveaway-easy manner. There is no recollection of what happened of the Shelters house.

Mongangane was 37 years old and Mahadi was pregnant with their fifth son, my father, when they moved to Viljoensdrif. Unfortunately, this meant that the family had to be broken up. Bernard, the fourth born, was taken to Libertas to live at Ou Chaane's house where Jerry, the eldest, already stayed. With not a lot of money in the kitty, the family could do with help from extended relatives and the support structure in Orange Free State was solid.

Shortly after arrival in Stofberg, Moses was born, and this meant more change in the family dynamics. Takatso remembered that when they were in Orlando, he, as the elder brother, was assigned to carrying Bernard on his back whenever they were out playing in the streets with other children. And now with Bernard gone, and a new baby in the house, the responsibility to carry Moses fell on Spanky.

Takatso told me he was relieved that it was not him. He had been frustrated a few times with Bernard who seemed to throw his tantrums just when the fun started for Takatso and the other children. 'He knew that all he needed to do was to cry for me to pick him up and carry him on my back. Bernard would stand behind me and wail until Mme came to hit me for not carrying him. So I would be standing there with Bernard on my back while others played.'

This passing on of sibling harmony was a clever tactic by the parents to instil a fraternal bond, the 'I've got your back' friendship nobody could break. They literally lived the mantra 'he ain't heavy, he's my brother', something they carried into adulthood.

The older Mofokeng boys, Takatso and Spanky, went to the primary school in Stofberg. Takatso remembered that the village was big, with houses built in rows. On the other side of the village was a boarding school for boys and girls, a teacher training college, the seminary and the primary school.

Going to Stofberg put Mongangane in a class of luminaries of the Black NG Kerk. Many years later, the name of the institution is revered in the hearts of the clergy and the older generations of the church. It symbolised prestige and the highest echelons of training for Black ministers and evangelists. They may not have been permitted to serve in the White NG Kerk, but they could write their own legacies in the Black church.

Stofberg-Gedenkskool (SGS), or Stofberg Memorial School in English, was opened on 1 October 1908 on the farm Elandsfontein in the northern Orange Free State. The nearest railway station was Viljoensdrif and the nearest town Heilbron.

The school was established jointly by the four NG Kerk synods of the Cape, Free State, Natal and Transvaal and was named after Dominee (Reverend) Pieter Stofberg, who had been an NG Kerk missionary in Mochudi, Botswana, from 1898 to 1907. Stofberg had actively campaigned for the establishment of a theological school for the NG Kerk mission but died in 1907 before seeing his dream realised.

The institution grew between 1935 and 1959, when numerous buildings were erected, and more students registered. The state subsidies helped Stofberg to cater for a large student number and their families. It took a Standard 4 to be admitted into the three-year evangelist course at Stofberg. That prerequisite was increased to Standard 6 when Mongangane got there.

He and his peers were under the tutelage of White Afrikaner male lecturers such as AM Hofmeyr, who was the director, AA Odendaal, LP Maree, Dr JA van Wyk and Dr AS van Niekerk. The theological training was diaconological and missiological. The first year was preparatory, and the rest comprised theological training.

Professor Klippies Kritzinger explained that the 'missionary theological education' of the NG Kerk had been rigidly separated. For White missionaries or *eerwaardes* (honourables), the *Sending-instituut* in Wellington in the Western Cape provided training from 1876 to 1962. By the time it was closed, it had produced 566 missionaries for the NG Kerk mission, which constituted 71 per cent of the total missionary work force of the church. The other 29 per cent was trained at Stellenbosch University and (later also) Pretoria University. These *eerwaardes* played a huge role in the NG Kerk mission in South (and southern) Africa.

Takatso said that in the evangelism class students were taught about inequality and its justifications: that the Boers had brought civilisation to Africa, had come here with a calling, and were like the Israelites. The assignment for the students was to evangelise their people to accept their lower status in society and assimilate into the Afrikaner culture where they would always be subservient. Kritzinger identified this arrangement as the root of racial separation in the church. Since the *eerwaardes* would 'only' work among Blacks, who were seen as inferior, they were not given the same theological formation as the NG Kerk ministers for White congregations. They weren't required to learn Greek and Hebrew, for instance. They could not be called to serve in White congregations or serve the sacraments in them. Even as visiting ministers, they were not allowed onto the pulpit.

On the other hand, the Theological Faculty at Stellenbosch has been training White ministers for over 160 years, equipping them with Greek and Hebrew and everything else required to be a 'proper' Reformed minister. It wasn't until 1999, that ministers of the URCSA were accepted at Stellenbosch University.

In other words, Blacks had always been serviced by 'underachievers', while Whites had their spiritual needs met by premium students.

The establishment of Stofberg was to train Black teachers in addition to evangelists and ministers. Interestingly, Kritzinger noted that two ecumenical visitors, Dr Norman Goodall and Reverend Eric W Nielsen, who made a survey of ministerial training in Africa for the International Missionary Council, commented that Stofberg-Gedenkskool was well staffed with five lecturers, including a recently appointed African tutor, and that it was one of the best equipped theological schools in the Union. The African tutor was a temporary lecturer, *Eerwaarde* Thomas Mahlangu, who taught an aspect of practical theology between 1954 and 1955.

But at the heart of it, Takatso tells me, Stofberg was started because the Boers in the Free State complained about the impact of the work of the trade unionist Clements Kadalie on their labourers. They were starting to see and feel the impact of trade unionism on their farms. Essentially institutions like Stofberg were opened to use religion to mitigate and counteract the impact of Kadalie's teachings. For this, Boers were prepared to reach into their pockets to make contributions towards the construction of the seminary and teacher training academy.

The religious training at Stofberg did nothing to integrate African culture into Western Christianity, and the students, like Mongangane, struggled to put the two together and to balance them.

Mahadi, as the wife of an evangelist, also attended classes. These were to provide in-service training to equip the spouses to become skilled preachers of the Word and leaders of the women ministries.

* * *

Takatso remembered the time at Stofberg fondly.

'There was a large number of ministers and evangelists in training. In the immediate opposite house was the Buti family, headed by the father of Sam Buti. We called Sam *aubuti* Oupa because he was like our eldest brother in that street. He had a younger sister called *ausi* Palesa and other siblings, Monyane, Mohlomi, and then Mokheseng the last born who was Moses's age. While I played with Mohlomi, Spanky was on duty looking after Moses who played with Mokheseng. The Buti family became closest to ours.'

Stofberg, located in the fertile area between Heilbron and Vereeniging, had an abundance of peach trees, every yard boasted a few. The oversupply of the fruit took Mahadi back to the Flip Heyns *huis* in Libertas where she had been groomed in the kitchen. Drying the peaches was the best way to make the bounty last. She went about the slog of skinning them, taking out the pit and then slicing them into halves or quarters.

The houses had thatched roofs. Mahadi placed the prepared peaches on corrugated iron sheets to dry in the warmth of the roof. Even in winter, the drying process worked well.

'But of course Spanky and I could not let the poor peaches dry peacefully.'

Takatso's expression became mischievous as he recalled. 'We would climb on chairs to help ourselves to mouthfuls of the peaches. Then one day, the sheet slipped and fell, sending the peaches tumbling and scattering all over the floor. We were too short to put everything back up, so we had to wait until our parents came back home to discover the accident. The least we could have done was to pick them up from the floor and neatly put them back in their rows on the sheet. But, man, we had to take a beating.

'Not that it stopped us. We carried on raiding the drying peaches in the warm roof. Even in the village when our trees were cleaned out, and the Butis had nothing left either, we would walk around the village stealing peaches until one day we got caught in somebody's garden. I was the first one to be caught and the man recognised me as Mofokeng's son. To get him off my back, I told him that my brother was also in the garden hiding among the trees. He told me to stand there while he went in search of Spanky, that's when I made off. Spanky had long skipped the yards and run back home. The man eventually came to our house to complain to our parents about our thieving ways, but it didn't work. For some reason, we never got lashings that one time.'

Stofberg was a close-knit community, where everybody knew everybody. The children played together and went to the same primary school. It was nothing out of the ordinary, therefore, that

Mongangane arranged with some of the students from the teacher training college to cut his sons' hair.

Takatso said the shaving was a traumatic experience.

'I never forgot that experience and I never liked it one bit. They used a razor, and it was quite uncomfortable. You sat there, literally on a knife's edge. One shake and the razor sinks into the scalp and leaves you dripping with blood. Our father left us no choice. We had to bear it and pray for the torture to end.'

Stofberg may have held a promise of a better life, but poverty still stared them in the face. As seminary students, Mongangane and others received rations from the school that included mealie meal, beans, salt and sugar, but no meat. With the little stipend he received, or from income from other sources, Mongangane bought meat. He rode to the butchery in Viljoensdrif on the road to Koppies using the bicycle he had bought in the village. He would return with *masapo* (bones) and *mala le mohodu* (tripe) meant to last a month.

There was quite a stretch between Stofberg and the town. Living off rations wasn't easy. Food had to be used sparingly and portions on the plate were never generous.

During holidays some families went away to visit relatives in towns and villages, but the Mofokengs stayed put for the full three years of training at Stofberg, enduring all difficulties until graduation.

Mongangane received an offer from the Gelukspan congregation, 350 kilometres away in the western Transvaal, and the family prepared to move. True to form, Mongangane did what he had done once before, when they'd left their home in Orlando, Soweto. This time he gave away most of the furniture the family had collected. Their only belongings, as they set off to start a new career in unknown lands, was a bed and a few loose items that could fit on the back of a small bakkie.

The Dreyers wanted Mongangane to be an evangelist in their community once he'd finished his studies. They knew that he was trained to inculcate the teachings of subservience to Blacks; to work hard, to reject alcohol and to accept low pay. The stance was decidedly anti-trade unionism, which advocated for better working conditions and salaries.

Takatso remembers his time when he was a young minister himself in Migdol (in today's North West) and how the White farmer would inform him who the lazy labourers were, who avoided work, and who drank too much. It would become his responsibility as the minister to approach the troublesome workers and persuade them to work hard and not demand high salaries, to stop drinking alcohol and beating their wives.

For people like Mongangane and his son Takatso, their duty was to serve the agenda of the Boer and ensure that his interests were protected.

* * *

Some seven years after the Mofokengs departed from Stofberg, its gates were shut. Its legacy, however, lives on.

The report of the Synodal Mission Commission that served before the 1957 Synod of the Transvaal NG Kerk described the circumstances of the time as follows: '... all three educational institutions (Stofberg Memorial School, Bethesda Normal School and Emmarentia Geldenhuys School) either closed or moved within five years because, according to the Group Areas Act, they were black spots or institutions in white areas.'

The report said after long negotiations with the Native Affairs Department the closures proved to be a necessity. It noted that nothing could be done through memoranda and negotiations with the Department, and all that was left was to seek where the schools could be moved to and how the church would still play its part in education in a way that would be most advantageous to it. The report further noted that the government had been very lenient, was always approachable and had served the management with the best advice.

As such, Stofberg Mountain Memorial School's Normal School students would be enrolled in state institutions such as at Thaba Nchu in the Free State and a possible training school in the district of Pietersburg (today's Polokwane, situated in Limpopo province).

It concluded that the state would welcome it if the church placed its institutions at its educational institutions for the good influence of its pupils and students. The church, on the other hand, would be grateful if it could use the state's educational institutions for the academic training of its theological students. The four Federated Churches decided to sell the land and buildings at Stofberg. And so the fate of Stofberg was sealed.

Kritzinger counted that in 1959 there were four lecturers and 120 students in the theological school when it had to relocate to a 'Bantu area'.

To that point, 84 ministers, 651 evangelists and about 1 100 fully trained teachers had graduated from the school.

Some of its most prominent alumni ministers are the Reverends SS Tema, ML Maile, W Xaluva and T Mahlangu. There were many more committed and devoted evangelists and ministers who made an indelible mark on communities but have been forgotten.

I hope, that in the telling of the story of my grandfather, I am able to help shine some light on the contributions of the unsung heroes that Stofberg produced.

People like Mongangane, who spent their lives serving their communities.

* * *

When Kritzinger paid tribute to the Stofberg seminary institution in his address to the URCSA synod, he urged that writing the history of Stofberg from the viewpoint of the receivers of the training would be 'to celebrate the generations of teachers, evangelists, women workers and ministers that the Stofberg-Gedenkskool and its successor institutions produced for the work of ministry in the NG Sendingkerk, NG Kerk in Afrika and eventually the URCSA'.

He accepted the racism, paternalism, alienation and exclusion that Black evangelists and ministers experienced in these institutions, the narrow and limited theological perspectives presented to them, as well as the subservience and conservatism transferred to them by the (almost exclusively White) group of lecturers. He said these should not be overlooked. However, he also urged people to celebrate the amazingly positive fruits that flowed from the experiences of groups of theological students eating, sleeping, studying, praying, quarrelling and playing together in the apartheid seminaries.

Kritzinger argued that more research was needed to unravel the past.

'The history of these 100 years needs to be written; we need to tell our own stories, we need to listen to everyone else's stories and write them down, especially our older colleagues (ministers, evangelists, women workers, who may not be with us much longer). A series of publications could flow from this, but maybe it could also serve the interest of reconciliation and construct a common past – so that we may have a common future.'

* * *

In my effort to retrace the steps of my family in Stofberg, I'm met by a behemoth called Groenpunt Maximum Correctional Facility on the R716 to Deneysville in the Free State. The officers insisted that it's not a prison, but a 'facility'.

My attempts to be granted permission to visit the site hit a few brick walls and left me bruised. What I have been told is that the old buildings and the once vibrant seminary and the village lined by peach trees were razed to make way for the incarceration facility managed by the Department of Correctional Services.

* * *

The bureaucrats refused me access on the grounds that no photography was allowed in correctional facilities. My pleas and petitions to be allowed access to observe what remains without photography went ignored.

It was a painful reminder of how we are often denied access to places of ancestral and historical significance. Whether it's on farms owned by descendants of Boers, where our forebears are buried, or sites run by government or private companies, it is never easy.

What happened with Stofberg is an aide-memoire that nothing is permanent in life. Hendrik Verwoerd, the ruthless native affairs minister and prime minister of South Africa, declared the holy grounds of Stofberg a White area some 70 years ago and closed the seminary down.

Today, with a majority population of Black men doing time, this place that was once a centre of prayer and faith, turned a White-privilege reserve, is now where murderers and rapists from the Free State serve lengthy and life sentences. As the only maximum-security prison in the province, it is notoriously overcrowded, with a high rate of recidivism (repeat offenders). There are reported violent deaths, riots, rapes, intimidation and dangerous gangs behind bars where life hangs precariously in the shadow of communicable diseases and viruses that lurk about.

Oh, the chilling irony of the circle of life!

8

In the lucky lake

The road to Gelukspan. PHOTO: AUTHOR

For over 100 kilometres, stretching from Lichtenburg in the north east to Khunwana in south west, tracts upon tracts of land known as the Trust have been owned and tilled by Black communities for generations. A look in the history books tells of the 1936 Native Trust (or Bantu Trust) and Land Act No. 18, which extended the land set aside for reserves from 7.3 per cent, as allocated by the infamous 1913 Native Land Act, to almost 13 per cent. It still forbade any ownership and/or purchase of land by natives outside the stipulated reserves and put Blacks under the watch of Native

Commissioners and Agricultural Officers. This made for a fertile ground of an unconventional Black South African experience in the Highveld area also known as Ditsobotla of present-day North West province.

This unique set of circumstances cultivated a self-sufficient and resourceful community. Apartheid engineers had put these Blacks in the Trust's settlements and reserves as part of their grand segregation project, but the oppressor inadvertently created an unorthodox class of independent Blacks who thrived in agriculture and amassed wealth over the years.

This is not to say that it was Shangri-La; they still faced a life of lack and limited opportunities typical of rural settlements. The twin issues of health and education remained arduous challenges, but with the absence of the White man to dictate their every move, people's lives were different.

* * *

The young White doctor ran as fast as he could while Ou Dikobe gave chase. His sjambok drew squiggly lines in the air as he snapped it and sunk its bite into the doctor's back, propelling him to run faster to outpace his geriatric assailant. Dikobe, frothing at the mouth with rage, did not let up. He shouted: '*Kom aan, baasie, jou klein stront!*', calling him a little rubbish for being lazy.

By the time he reached the parking lot, and with throngs of amused bystanders doubled over with laughter at this unusual attack, the White doctor was out of breath and relieved by the intervention of the uniformed Gelukspan Hospital security personnel.

Dikobe had gone on the offensive because he believed the recalcitrant young man needed to be herded back to the hospital grounds, in the same way Dikobe herded his donkeys when they went missing in the wild.

Dikobe, from the village of Lombardslaagte, had grown impatient and restless in the casualty department after he had brought his critically ill granddaughter in a donkey cart to the hospital only to be informed that the doctor was at home in the staff quarters having tea. With the girl at death's door, he could wait until she died on his watch, or he could do what any good grandparent would do – save her life. And so Dikobe chose the latter. He disappeared into the complex with his sjambok and came out driving the White doctor before him.

This incident that Takatso remembered well, may have been a source of fun banter at the time – something out of an unrealistic episode of the 'Days of the Lives of Black People at a Time of Apartheid' – but it laid bare the power that Blacks wielded in the Trust area. The presence of a White man was of no real consequence to them. It was only when they ventured into town that things became real and they were 'put in their place' quickly.

'The issue of oppression in the area of Gelukspan did not arise, it did not exist,' Takatso who lived in Gelukspan between 1952 and the early 1970s told me.

The young doctor was only the third White man in the area, the others being Dominee Ferreira, who also lived in the hospital complex, and Streak, the shopkeeper in the neighbouring village of Uitkyk.

This is how Takatso explained it: 'Apartheid was not only simply about the relationship between Black and White, it was an urban problem. In that whole area of the Trust, there were no White people to give instructions to those Blacks. The communities never depended on government. The people had their own wells and lands, and they were resourceful. They got on with life and made do with what they had. Here was Ou Dikobe who knew that this White man was a baasie (little boss), but he could go to his house and whip him – a White doctor – all the way back to work. That was unimaginable in other places in the 1960s.

'These were independent and well-to-do, hard-working Black people with initiative. Africans who created opportunities for themselves. They had no chief, only a headman, and a commissioner in Lichtenburg overseeing their affairs. Even when they went to Lichtenburg, they walked into the *kooperasie winkel* (co-operative store), put money on the table, and drove out with their tractor or whatever they needed.

'The summer harvest was a carnival in Gelukspan. The farmers would span oxen and draw a trailer full of fresh produce like mealies, pumpkin, sugar cane and watermelon, and head out to the city of Mafeking (now Mahikeng) and they would return with handsome amounts of money after a week or two. They were feeding the people in town and the surrounding villages that couldn't produce vegetables and fruit.

'So these Black people never experienced oppression, subjugation and control while living in the Trust. They remained independent and resilient with their own resources and, with the money earned, they sent their children to schools. They didn't work for White people. It's only their children who left to work in the towns for White people. In my time, we didn't go to town to look for work. We went there to buy what we needed or to sell our produce.'

Change crept in with the passage of time and Takatso located it in the unpredictable cycles of the weather and population growth.

'The scales were tipped by the natural cycles of agriculture, the good and the bad years of rain and drought. The people in the Trust ultimately weakened and some lost their independence and power. The land didn't increase but people's numbers did, so their children could not get land and they had to go to school and look for work from White people. Their exposure to the urban economy changed power relations and they became subservient and had to learn how to say baas, something foreign to them because in the world they grew up in, baas was whipped with a sjambok. Now the tables had turned – baas was the one whipping them into line.

'We were a free people. We had seen Ou Dikobe whipping a White man with a sjambok. One time, the son of Streak, the shopkeeper, hit Moses, my younger brother, and I heard about it. I went straight into the shop and beat this young boy up. I didn't recognise him as White or superior to me. I saw a young boy who hit my brother and I needed to discipline him, (and I could do that) without fear that I would be arrested or the Whites would gang up on me.

'I only became conscientised when I got to Emmarentia High School (near Warmbaths, now known as Bela Bela). I even got expelled. It was an awakening to realise that this country was not ours. Having grown up in Gelukspan, I didn't know what apartheid was,' said Takatso.

It was interesting that my aunt Tshidiso had a different take on Streak. She remembered him as a racist who would not allow them to use his toilets and was disgusted by them speaking Setswana in his store. He insisted that the medium of communication be Afrikaans. Tshidiso's account dated a few years after Takatso left Gelukspan for boarding school. Could it be that Streak hardened in the time that Takatso was at Emmarentia High School?

* * *

Takatso left me energised with this account of life in Gelukspan. I had been oblivious to certain aspects. I knew that the people were resourceful and that farming and agriculture formed the backbone of this area, but somehow the proud stories of chutzpah and resilience were never told enough. What stood out for me was disease, especially tuberculosis, and the poverty, both of which are well-recorded in studies.

In his doctoral thesis titled 'Progress Towards Health For All in the Gelukspan Health Ward – 1985', Dr Marthinus Bac presented a dire picture of a disintegrating social fabric in the late 1970s and early 1980s Gelukspan, where he worked at the time.

He reported that a 1983 annual report of the Gelukspan Community hospital indicated that infections and nutrition-related diseases were very common. Among preschool children diarrhoeal disease, respiratory tract infections and malnutrition were the major killers.

Tuberculosis was the most important infectious disease with a high case mortality among adults. Hypertension and its complications accounted for the majority of deaths in the medical wards.

In 1984, there were 451 known psychiatric patients in the district. The most common diagnosis made was schizophrenia (54 per cent) followed by alcoholic psychosis (10 per cent) and dementia (7.5 per cent). There were 423 known epileptics in the district.

He reported that in 1980, around 8 per cent of the men who had a pre-school child were unemployed. Of the men who had a job, three quarters worked in South Africa (as opposed to the Bophuthatswana Bantustan), and did not live at home. About 30 per cent of the mothers in the area had paid jobs, mostly as live-in domestic workers. They did not stay at home and more than half of them came home less than once a week.

More detail from Bac's thesis reveals that some 40 per cent of households with pre-school children possessed land in 1980 and ploughed at the average 10 morgen. Most people owned animals, usually cattle, sheep, goats, horses, donkeys, pigs and chickens.

Bac added surveys had found out that 88.4 per cent of the households lived in their own houses, which mostly consisted of more than four rooms built out of bricks. Only 10 per cent of these could access electricity. Wood, paraffin, cow dung and coal were used as fuel for cooking and heating the houses. Candles and paraffin lamps were used to light homes in the evenings.

* * *

The Mofokeng family arrived in Gelukspan in 1952.

This is the year when Mongangane set up a home there with his industrious wife Mahadi. In tow were Takatso, the second born, who became the erudite book worm, Spanky, the headstrong third born, who would eventually join the police force, and Moses, the last born, who had an entrepreneurial spirit.

The other two sons; Jerry, the first born, who would become an evangelist like his father, and Bernard the benign fourth born who would become a civil servant, were left in the care of extended family in the Orange Free State, as happened in many African families – for practical reasons – at the time.

Bernard became so accustomed to life on the farms that when Takatso was sent to fetch him to re-join his family he refused, opting for a life behind a tractor. It would take him a while to come to Gelukspan.

The family welcomed its only daughter in 1953 when they adopted the two-year-old Tshidiso, the daughter of Mongangane's younger sister, Mapiletsa, the same sister who had taunted Mahadi as a young bride in the Orange Free State.

Tshidiso went on to become a teacher.

Gelukspan is the place where our family solidified itself.

Mongangane was the rock at its foundation, and his determination to make something of life and to do good would be reflected in the family and in the broader community he had come to work in. He was conscientious, thorough and steadfast.

9

Construction site

In 1959, Takatso was 10 years old, Spanky was eight, and my father, Moses, was just three when their parents began a missionary career as fresh graduates from Stofberg-Gedenkskool of the NG Kerk in Afrika.

The story goes that the place they had arrived in was named Gelukspan after a wanderer, long ago, walking along the pan, or a small lake in the area, discovered a diamond. The Dutch-speaking farmers who'd already settled there called it Gelukspan then, the word 'geluk' having the dual meaning of 'happy' and 'lucky' in Afrikaans. Further probing yielded no gains, however, so the luck was short-lived. The diggings are still there, standing as evidence of this flash in the pan.

Gelukspan is known for its dry climate, with a summer rainfall of 400 to 600 millimetres a year and a dry winter that lasts from May to September. The area is part of the so-called maize-triangle and is suitable for the cultivation of maize, sorghum, sunflowers, beans and groundnuts. The landscape is flat, with fields for grazing, and bushveld apart from cultivated areas.

Takatso, though older than the other two, is the only one of the three boys who went to Gelukspan who could tell me what this new world was like, since Spanky and Moses are no longer alive.

The place was an arid cattle post. It was nothing like the bright city lights of Johannesburg, or the busy and restless streets of Orlando in Soweto. Neither was it the vibrant Stofberg where his father Mongangane had attended missionary school. This was Gelukspan, the lucky pan with not much happening.

The area was divided into three groups of villages: traditional, Trust and resettlements. Researchers note that the traditional villages or old reserves for the Black population originated many decades earlier when the Molopo and Setlagole reserves were allocated to some Tswana tribes by the Boers after they had fought together against Mzilikazi. Some of these villages have been in existence since before 1900.

In the 1940s, as the architects of apartheid implemented their grand scheme of segregation, they purchased the land of Afrikaner/ Dutch farmers under the Bantu Trust and Land Act, Act No.18 of 1936. Groups of Black people were settled on these farms – Trust lands, as they became known – which had names such as Goedgevonden, Lombardslaagte, Naauwpoort, Nooitgedacht, Schoongezicht, Springbokpan and Weltevreden.

The resettlements came later, in the 1970s, and were made up of people removed from 'Black spots' and Black townships and farms.

The land was flat as far as the eye could see. The prospect of a lively community life seemed minimal. The villages were spread out and the distances between them were such that you needed a bicycle to get from one to the other. People had to walk far to visit one another.

Dominee Ferreira, the first missionary to arrive in Gelukspan, two years before the Mofokengs, was kind enough to fetch the family from the train station in Sannieshof with his bakkie. With their few items they walked into an old house. Aged as it was, and tearing at the seams, it had maintained its Victorian charm with its creaking wooden floors and pressed ceilings. It would do for the family.

Takatso remembered: 'We got there to an old house that looked like it was owned by a White family. It was built out of stones. There was one room without wooden flooring that became the pantry. It was called the *pakkamer* and was used for lashings. That's where we were taken for a good beating. Our father would never ask our mother what we did wrong, he just got home and Mme would say 'Chapatso, *nchapele bana ba na'* (beat these children for me). All he would say is: *'Pakkamer toe'* (to the *pakkamer*) and we would head down the corridor to the dreaded room where we knew we were in for a good cry.

'Spanky was tougher and didn't cry easily. I figured out that the longer it took us to cry, the longer our father would keep lashing. He would not let up until Mme said it was enough. I knew that letting out a cry would bring her in to ask for him to spare us. So it took a few seconds and I would start wailing and Mme would rush in to intervene.'

As an aside, the word *pakkamer*, literally means 'room where things are packed', but the Afrikaans word for a lashing or a hiding is pak. The room was well named: the room where you got your *pak*.

* * *

I found out from Takatso that Mongangane had picked the distant Gelukspan because he disliked the idea of working among his own people.

'He wanted to go far away. One day towards the completion of his training he visited home at Madraereng in the Orange Free State and went to pass his greetings to the baas. The man ordered him to return to his family to evangelise. He knew in his heart that would never happen. He returned at a later time to inform the baas that he had opted to go to Gelukspan in the district of Lichtenburg and there was nothing they could do. And that's how he left his family and avoided being an evangelist among his own people, choosing a strange land.'

It was also probably a Biblical decision too, based on the scriptures about how a prophet is rejected in his hometown because of familiarity or scepticism. Gelukspan presented a challenge Mongangane could relish.

Takatso said when Mongangane got to Gelukspan he found some converts already who were not 'church people' as they had had no shepherd for many years. These people, some of whom were first-generation Christians, had encountered the religion through missionaries in their places of origin. They were staunch believers with a conservative disposition. His job was to revive these Christians who were despondent in spirit and needed to hear the message of Jesus Christ, the Redeemer. Mongangane embarked on a massive project to bring them into the organised church. This put him as the only resident Black evangelist in a large area spanning over 100 kilometres from west to east and 60 kilometres from north to south.

'Ntate reintroduced the messages of Jesus Christ as a saviour of people and reminded believers to have hope beyond this life. The people knew about the afterlife but that message had been lost to them after years of not having a messenger of hope. Ntate's presence brought a message of revival as he re-established a living church,' Takatso said.

The other churches in the area at that time were the Wesleyan in nearby Bapong, and the Lutheran in Bodibe, some 30 kilometres or so away. Going deeper south to Khunwana there were no churches. The ministers for these other denominations lived in towns and seldom came to deliver the holy communion. Dominee Ferreira was *lekgowa* (a White man) whom they couldn't relate to as much as they did to Mongangane. Whatever events happened in the area – funerals, parties, weddings – they knew that Evangelist Mofokeng would be there for them. Gelukspan stood out as an oasis of faith due to his presence and he got stitched into the fabric of the community as one of them.

Without a church structure in place, the new congregants, about a dozen, gathered in a storeroom of the *ou huis* every Sunday, sitting on benches singing from *Lifela tsa Sione*. Some of them were Basotho with strong ties to the Orange Free State and Lesotho, and as such bonds were created among the folk and the Mosotho evangelist.

* * *

Outside the church, the family had to adjust and get on with life. And for the 10-year-old Takatso and eight-year-old Spanky it presented a few bumps.

Takatso said they went to the primary school in nearby Uitkyk village and attended in an old structure, which he suspected must have been used as a school for the White farm children before the arrival of the Trust and resettlements. The building was derisively called Jan van Riebeek by the locals.

'Like all other children we had illnesses. We were poor. I didn't have shoes in the whole three years that we were in Stofberg. And I loved soccer and when my feet itched I would kick whatever was in sight. As a result, I kicked stones, bottles, glasses and other things that actually harmed me. I became a regular at the clinic and both my feet carry scars from all the cuts and gashes.

'As children we had to learn a new language. Imagine, we were from Orlando, where we spoke Sesotho and isiXhosa, and in Stofberg we spoke Sesotho. From there we had to speak Setswana in Gelukspan. We were already of school-going age and had been taught in Sesotho throughout. We walked to school in Uitkyk barefoot and played with Batswana children. We came from the city of Johannesburg, lived in the peri-urban Stofberg, and now we found ourselves in a totally rural African area in the western Transvaal, with only two White people in the entire place, Dominee Ferreira and Streak, the English shop owner in Uitkyk.'

* * *

In no time, there were signs of life in Gelukspan because of Mongangane's resourcefulness. A clinic was opened inside the *ou huis* after an agreement between the church and Mongangane. The Mofokengs opened the doors of their abode to welcome the sickly and to administer treatment. One of the rooms was turned into an out-patient department and the next was where the nurse lodged. Mapanana Bojosi was the first nurse, and she brought along her daughter Dudu. A Doctor de Jager from Sannieshof came to see patients every Friday.

The healthcare facility attracted patients from near and far, and some would be stranded for transport back home and would then squeeze themselves in the Mofokeng children's bedrooms.

'Mapanana was succeeded by a nurse from Mafikeng who drank. Her name escapes me,' said Takatso. 'Then came MaRampa who eventually moved to Botswana, and her children are still our close friends. She was followed by Susan Nkeng Molamu who lived with her husband Shepstone Molamu. At the time of Susan, a new structure was built by the church and the nurse did not have to lodge in the *ou huis*.'

Not that the Mofokeng family was left alone to enjoy their privacy. The foot traffic remained consistent, with desperate travellers who had missed the 5 pm bus to Mafeking or Lichtenburg seeking overnight shelter there.

The clinic that was developed to become Gelukspan Hospital.
This photograph was taken in 1958. PHOTO: FAMILY ALBUM

With the clinic and the church becoming popular, the area started showing signs of potential for development. It had become a meeting point for travellers and for different cultures. The bus to Lichtenburg in the Transvaal picked up passengers near the clinic, while the bus to Mafeking, which was in the Cape Province then (it is now part of the province known as the Northern Cape), dropped them off. This intersection of the bus routes would eventually bear fruit with all the traffic in transit.

* * *

A magnificent church, built in typical NG Kerk style of a steeple-chase mounted by a cock and the cardinal signs, soon went up, and stood then as a testament not only to my grandfather's commitment to his faith and his people, but also to his physical work.

The building brought some excitement in the Reserve. Its large champagne-coloured stained windows gave it the allure and distinction of the White churches seen in some of the exclusive White suburbs that barred Black Christians from walking through their doors. It was with the generous contributions from the congregants and donations from the *Moederkerk* (mother church) that the project got off the ground.

With their hands, the congregation and architects, led by Mongangane, laid the foundation. The scaffolding went up, and a modern church with fine finishings of wooden flooring, oak benches with back rests, stained windows and a church bell that could echo tens of kilometres away, stood tall.

The newly completed church in 1958. PHOTO: FAMILY ALBUM

In a 2004 interview for the *Sunday Times*, Mongangane told me: 'I practically laid the foundation, ran the concrete-making machine and formed the bricks. There is not a single iron sheet I didn't touch when we roofed the building. You see the fence that runs around the church – it was also put up by me.'

In outlying villages, congregants gathered in people's houses or in schools for Sunday service, and Mongangane made it his priority to build proper church structures. He erected these churches in seven villages and a few more elsewhere in the Lichtenburg district.

To replicate the success of this community collaboration, the ambitious project of building a hospital got underway. This time, the church community donated money and contributed with their labour once more. There was also a grant from the Biesiesvlei Mission Committee of the *Moederkerk*.

Mongangane effectively became the project manager, foreman and supervisor. He had to organise the programme and schedule of labour, liaising with church elders across the villages of Lichtenburg Reserve. He would climb on his scooter – the mode of transport he came to use in later years – to inform the teams about their turn on the building schedule and ensure that enough hands reported for duty and that everything ran on time every week.

Mantlaletseng Morobe met Mongangane when she was a teen. Now in her 80s, soft spoken and gentle, she remembered those days of activity fondly.

'For the building of the church, they used to collect stones, using *dikotoko* (a long sleigh) filled with stones and drawn by 12 oxen. Ntate Mofokeng and my father would offload and then go back for more. It was hard labour when you think about it. They were not paid as everyone pitched in for the community.

'The same hard labour went into the building of the clinic and the hospital, digging and putting brick to mortar. Ntate Mofokeng lived right next to the hospital, and became the effective supervisor who led the community from the front. He was great as a leader.

He was meticulous and precise when he did the stocktaking of the deliveries of stones, sand, cement, the ceiling, and all the building material needed to ensure that construction was never disrupted or delayed.'

I remembered Ezekiel Lebotse as a tall and imposing man with a trimmed moustache who became a close family friend. When I met him, decades later, he showed no sign of slowing down. The moustache is still there, completely White. His long, gesticulating hands moved animatedly as he reminisced about Mongangane.

'Ntate Mofokeng was the leader in the building of the hospital. I'm not telling you hearsay, I was there. He built the church first with *dikotoko*. After finishing the church he moved on to build the first three blocks of the hospital and then he brought in the White contractors.

'He also had a direct hand in the building of other churches outside Gelukspan where he worked – places such as Biesiesvlei, the church in Lichtenburg on the main road, and Bospoort near GaMaloka.'

Reminiscing about the massive construction site at Gelukspan, Takatso said they formed bricks and pushed wheelbarrows. Mongangane mixed concrete with a shovel.

'I for one was a *dagaboy* (a young man mixing cement and concrete) when I came home for the holidays from boarding school. My brothers Spanky and Moses, who were older by then, also worked on the construction site. My mother was at home cooking meals for the different shifts. After a long day of back-breaking labour we would all retire to the family house.

'We never knew a home where it was just my mother, father, Spanky, Moses and myself. Every day of our lives we lived with other people and that's what we knew a home to be. It never changed until my mother died.'

* * *

At the end of the hospital project, a few years later, the sprawling complex of Gelukspan had sprung up to add a new landmark on the otherwise flat, uninspiring and dull landscape of the Reserve. Dr Bac's thesis gives us more insight into the inner workings of the hospital buildings.

'In 1959 the clinic had 20 beds. During the 1960s a whole new hospital was built with 1 100 beds, including a general hospital, maternity ward, TB hospital, an institution for the chronically ill and the physically handicapped, and an old age home. At the same time, Tlamelang Special School for special education for the physically handicapped children plus hostels were built on the same premises. The facilities in the hospital were further improved with a new theatre block, a bigger laundry, a boiler house, a mortuary and more houses built for the hospital staff.'

Bac noted that the hospital never had more than one or two doctors on its staff and it rendered only hospital-based curative services. Patients with tuberculosis were referred there from a large area in the Northern Cape and western Transvaal. Chronically ill and handicapped patients were referred from all the provinces of South Africa, as far as the cities of Port Elizabeth and Cape Town.

'The fusion of religion and health care resulted in a holistic patient care as the ministers, evangelists and elders of the NG Kerk who lived in the same complex in the hospital supplemented the treatment as prescribed by the medical team with a dose of the gospel,' said Bac.

Bac estimated that about 50 villages over a 2 500 square kilometre area were serviced by Gelukspan Hospital. The population census of 1980 put the number of people then at 66 097. In 1985, the population had increased to 86 604.

The population profile of the district shows an expansive population with a high proportion of children and a high natural increase rate of 3.1 per cent. About 16 per cent of the population were children below five years of age, while 45 per cent were below 15. Less than 5 per cent were older than 65.

The most distant clinic from the hospital was about 90 kilometres away. Due to the uneven distribution of villages in the district, 75 per cent of the people stayed more than 50 kilometres from the hospital.

According to Dr Bac's thesis, by 1977 Gelukspan Hospital boasted multiple facilities:
- a maternity ward with 30 beds
- general wards for medical, surgical, gynaecological and psychiatric patients with 90 beds
- paediatric wards with 90 beds
- tuberculosis wards with 400 beds
- an institution for the physically handicapped with 320 beds
- an old age home with 80 beds
- a children's home
- an outpatient department
- a theatre with basic equipment and instruments
- an X-ray department
- an occupational therapy department
- four fixed clinics – small four-roomed buildings. Only three were staffed with a total staff of four registered nurses
- a mobile clinic that operated one or two days a week from the outpatient department
- a small fleet of relatively new vehicles (two lorries, three ambulances, two combis and numerous other cars).

The staff compliment was:
- one doctor helped by one or two army doctors
- about 300 nurses – fewer than 20 were registered nurses or midwives
- no qualified paramedical staff at all
- only assistants in the X-ray department, pharmacy and occupational therapy department
- a hospital administrator with a good number of clerks and other support staff in the maintenance department, laundry, kitchen and stores.

By any measure, it was a bustling place that launched careers and birthed superstars. I always brag that the most famous person who was born at Gelukspan Hospital is Tshepo Seate, who is better known as Stoan from the internationally renowned Afro-pop band Bongo Maffin. His family lived in the Trust village of Vrede. He was born there in 1975 and went on to become a force to be reckoned with in music, proving that there's more to Gelukspan than just agriculture and farming.

10
The making of a leader

Evangelist Mongangane Mofokeng in the late 1960s, standing extreme right in a black waistcoat, as chairman of Phalane Committee that ran Gelukspan Hospital. PHOTO: FAMILY ALBUM

Takatso beamed with pride when he recalled his father's work ethic. 'Ntate was a real missionary, dedicated and totally committed,' he says.

He pointed out that religion was already in the Mofokeng household with his grandfather Takatso, after whom he was named, the first to convert and who became an elder in the African Methodist Episcopal Church (AME). Having started his evangelism in his own home and winning his mother over, Mongangane had the energy and zeal to charge ahead with his missionary work in strange lands.

In the early days of his work, the church gave him a bicycle that he pedalled across the length and breadth of the Lichtenburg Reserve, from as far as the village of Sheila in the east, about 30 kilometres from Gelukspan, to the far west in Middleton, about 50 kilometres from Gelukspan, on the other side of Khunwana.

His mode of transport was upgraded with the arrival of the formidable pair of Rob and Rox drawing a cart made out of steel. The dark fillies became trusted companions for a few years until they were retired due to old age.

Moving with the times and embracing the popularity of motorcycles, probably because of speed, Mongangane began an era that would earn him a title for life and cemented his legacy as Mmoledi (evangelist), or Moruti (minister), wa Sekuta (on a scooter). This exciting piece of transportation had its cool factor and attracted attention.

Jerry remembered the motorbike as a DKW two-stroke RT 125 model manufactured in Germany. The auto maker, Dampf-Kraft-Wagen, founded in 1916, is known as an ancestor of the Audi company of today. From the 1920s until World War II, DKW was the biggest manufacturer of motorbikes. The company became defunct in 1966.

I remember us as children playing in old disused vehicles in Gelukspan. There was a rusty electric blue motorbike that we used to toss around – by then so much of it missing that it was really light, almost as light as a bicycle. I did not comprehend its importance and place in history. To us, it was an abandoned and rusty piece of machinery which, we were told, our grandfather used to ride.

Seetso Moremong had a better appreciation. He chose his words carefully as he dusted off the cobwebs in his memory to remember his earliest encounters with Mongangane. The most he could approximate was that he was a little boy growing up in Bapong village when the scooter became a legend of the platteland – a word that literally means 'flat land'.

He said it would kick up white dust past the north eastern side of the village as Mongangane approached the graveyard situated by the side of the road. The tiny engine made a buzzing noise to announce his imminent appearance from across the landscape. Curious onlookers with not much to excite them would stand by their doors or closer to the fence to watch this wonder of automation as it zoomed past, eliciting squeals of delight from the children who were in a frenzy. With everybody in the village calling the man on the scooter Ntate Mmoledi, the then ten-year-old Moremong assumed that Mmoledi was his name. It was later that he learned that it was his title.

Tshidiso, the Mofokengs' adopted daughter, remembered that Mongangane travelled as far as Botswana with the scooter to visit a family friend, Ntate Twala. On one of the trips, he skidded in the sandy desert dunes and sustained a leg injury that left a permanent scar. As soon as he recovered, he was back in the saddle.

Mongangane's generation of evangelists didn't have many opportunities and they were poorly paid. Most went on foot or rode bicycles. That he could afford a scooter was a big deal. On top of that, after the scooter gave in, he was able to upgrade.

He had saved enough to buy himself his first car, a second-hand white Ford Cortina. On the wrong side of 50, he took driving lessons and acquired his licence, earning him some respect in the streets of the Reserve, even among the Whites in town. With his speaking fluent Afrikaans, dressed smartly in a three-piece suit and a tie – and now driving a car – the Whites would mistake him for one of the rich Blacks from the Reserve. Mongangane always shared the story of how he would always politely disabuse them and explain that he was just a mere boer – a farmer.

When I visited Ezekiel Lebotse, he grew energetic and jumped in his sofa as he remembered the early days of the Ford Cortina.

'He made me laugh once when he came to complain about how difficult it was to control the car. He said it often lost its grip on the road and he would clutch on to the steering wheel so hard he dripped sweat. I knew the problem was the braking system. I took one of the parts out and showed him what he needed to replace when he had enough money. He came after a few days and I offered to install the parts. The problem was fixed and he left a happy customer. I didn't want him to pay me as I was helping my father out and he never ceased praising me as a mechanic.'

* * *

With such a vast area of coverage, Mongangane spent a lot of time on the road and became an absent husband to his wife and a missing father to his sons. It was like Orlando all over again. For him to preach at the Sunday service in a far-away village, he would have to leave home on a Saturday afternoon and return on Sunday night. During the Good Friday services he would be gone for the whole ten-day period.

His community leadership projects kept piling up – running the hospital, chairing school governing bodies and doing church administration. He was a man in demand.

Lebotse recounted: 'He was the chairman of the council called Phalane that ran the affairs of the hospital and the community working there. He headed the disciplinary committee also and would preside over hearings. They were merciful, they didn't actually expel people from work. They were more compassionate and more than anything they would have stern words for you to change your ways, without compromising you financially.

'Ntate Mofokeng saw the hospital grow as the leader of Phalane and on the other hand ran the church. I was elected an elder in the church council under his tutelage. He was the senior evangelist, assisted by Ntate Tholo, a Mopedi man from the North (now Limpopo province).

'I became their assistant, praying for patients. There were speakers that ran across the wards and the shop, so our prayers were broadcast across the hospital complex. I worked for three months. Ntate Tholo was slow and I was faster, and Tholo didn't like it that much. Ntate Mofokeng then deployed me to attend to church matters in villages such as Diretsane and Weltevreden. I became his travel companion on his scooter and then later in the Cortina.

'As the chairman of the school governing body (SGB) at Uitkyk Primary School, which is now known as Reitsositse Primary School, he led the construction of the new school. We collected money to extend the building of the school and Jan van Riebeek (the old school building) got demolished as new classes went up. I was against the idea because that building should have been left standing as a reminder of the apartheid school that only catered for the Boers who farmed in the area before we got re-settled here.'

Moremong told me this: 'Outside of the church and the hospital, I know that Ntate Mofokeng was influential in the building of several schools in the district. As the SGB chairman, he ensured the smooth running of these facilities. His strength seemed to lie in the ability to get people to pull together. When the community needed a school, they didn't have to petition the department of education. Ntate Mofokeng would be the first to agitate for change and the community would soon be sold and in a few years' time a brand new school would be standing. He loved education and the community listened to him, that is why he would always be voted in as the chairman of the SGB. At one point, he sat on the board of the district as the chairman of schools. That's how powerful he was.'

Mongangane opening a school. PHOTO: FAMILY ALBUM

Mantlaletseng Morobe's eyes twinkled behind her black-rimmed spectacles as she spoke.

'Ntate Mofokeng was the chairman of Uitkyk Primary School. He used to visit the schools around the area to pray or host meetings. He used to wake up early to do the rounds at the hospital praying for the ill. He worked for the souls of people, that man of God.

'He developed this place of Gelukspan and always spoke that

this hospital should belong to the community. When there was a disagreement over the hospital some years back, when the new government wanted to shut it down, we had to go to his home in Lotlhakane village where he retired. We invited him to address the MEC and the government officials at the hospital. The entire population of the Reserve came to hear for themselves. It was through his speech that Gelukspan hospital was saved. If it wasn't for him it might have been demolished because they were determined to close it down.'

With everyone I spoke to, there was general agreement that, even with all the demands on his time, Mongangane played all his roles well.

Moremong looked out of his window as if to find the right words: 'He did a great job of encouraging people to be religious and to attend the new church in the hospital complex. I was staying with my grandmother, Lydia Ramothibe, in Bapong at that time, and she was a member of the Methodist Church. She was visually impaired and my job as a grandson was to take her to church. I was soon conflicted because of the influence of the young people at the NG Kerk, especially my friend and neighbour Jasi Morobe, who belonged there. It seemed to be more alive and the atmosphere exceptionally exuberant. I was so taken that I joined the church. In 1977, Ntate Mofokeng taught me the catechism class and the following year I joined MBB (the church's youth ministry). I never looked back since then.'

Moremong remembered how famous Mongangane had become in the community. It was not only his hands-on approach and the personal touch he brought in his work, but he was a keen listener and observer and everyone warmed to him easily.

'He was interested in the wellbeing of people and freely associated with others from different denominations. He never kept to himself and his church. As such he became a father to all without prejudice or bias. I learned how to be a people's person from him.

'One of his greatest traits was the ability to organise and mobilise. He could rally people towards a common cause because his power of persuasion was unmatched. He was charismatic. He was also organised and orderly in his work space. He could have been a teacher. In fact, as a preacher of the Word, he was a teacher. He travelled far and wide across the district reaching some of the remotest villages no one ever ventured to visit. He always found a way to navigate the muddy terrain, the thorny back routes and the unpassable tracks, just so that he could reach the people and do God's work.

'He organised the congregation of Lichtenburg Reserve, which was made up of up to 12 or 13 wards. Hundreds upon hundreds of people would descend into the recreational hall of the hospital. It took real skill and flair to pull off an event of that magnitude when you consider what goes into it – collecting the money, transportation, accommodation, catering – and still ensuring that people were revived at the end of the three-day summit. The highlight was always the Saturday night vigil and, after the official proceedings, he would hand over the programme to the youth ministry.

'He was physically strong and he loved farming. The church had five morgen of land that he would work on. Life was different then and it took long hours of hard labour and sweat under the scorching sun as he weeded the crops with a hoe. There was none of the technology of today that has made things so much easier. When the going got tougher out in the fields he proved equal to the task, if not tougher. The congregation would then benefit from his hard work as we shared the mealies, sunflower or *mabele* (sorghum) that would be harvested.'

Morobe offered: 'Ntate Mofokeng was active. Never lazy. He did his work diligently, whether chairing a school committee meeting or praying for the patients. He did his work with passion. He was invested in the community and the schools. There is no doubt that he worked for this community. If it were possible, he should be raised from the dead to continue the amazing work he did for the people. We need his kind of leadership and skill, but his time has come and gone. He was known for his gentleness and kind heart, always ready to laugh.'

* * *

When it came to preaching, Mongangane was revered.

Moremong recalled: 'He was a powerful preacher. A man anointed and ordained by God. His sermons brought you closer to God. His knowledge and interpretation of the Bible was vast and it had depth. He made it all easy to understand because he always did his homework and prepared. That's why his sermons always landed so well on the congregation.

'In his efforts to build the church and entrench new Christian ways of life and culture, Ntate Mofokeng made sure that we honoured the day of Pentecost that followed the 40 days of the resurrection of Jesus. He would invite families to come to church to pray as we awaited the holy spirit. The numbers were really low in the beginning, but he persisted. He never got discouraged. He knew what he was doing was not for his glory but for the kingdom of God. Ntate Mofokeng worked to save our souls and for us to know God. Let it never be forgotten. Ascension Day is no longer a public holiday in South Africa but it's important for us never to lose sight and to always mark that day. If he was still around, he would have called us up to the house of the Lord to pray while we await the return of the holy spirit.

Mongangane, wearing spectacles, leads a hymn along with co-evangelist Ntate Tholo. Photo: Family Album

'He always read Psalm 27:10: *le ha mme le ntate ba ka ntahla, Jehova o tla nthola* ('Though my father and mother forsake me, the Lord will receive me'). His life became all about the Bible and preaching.

'His style of preaching was educational and informative. He would introduce you to the text and give you the history and context of that place and time and then apply it to practical everyday life of today, so that you could understand your place in the Word. Then he concluded with a summary and a reminder of the takeaway points from the verse. He supplemented his sermon with a moving prayer, capable of shaking mountains really, with his full and loud voice calling on Jehovah. Ntate Mofokeng pulled people towards God with the great and rare talent of a motivator.'

Morobe reminisced: 'He was a prized preacher. He loved the hymn *Jo Lefifi Le Lekaakang* ('Oh What Darkness Upon the World') and *Lona Ba Ratang Ho Phela* ('Those Who Long to Be in the Flock of Jesus'), in reference to the spirit of the people who were lost.

'He was a talented preacher and one of his favourite sermons was the story of Nicodemus, who went in the dark of the night, seeking salvation and a better life, to find Jesus. Jesus told him that he needed to be born again to see heaven. When you want to work for God you have to start again and shun earthly things and strive for the things of heaven. That was Ntate Mofokeng, yes. He showed us the way and built our faith.'

Lebotse agreed: 'He was a preacher par excellence. His word reverberated in our heads and would be recorded in our hearts and souls for days after his sermons. He was skilful. We would meditate on what he said – that's a mark of a great orator and preacher man. He had a God-given talent. He had a spirit anointed by God. And he lived a godly life and stayed true to his calling, preaching to people and putting us in the right path.'

* * *

Away from the pulpit, Mongangane had to show strength and Moremong described him as such: 'He was an unflinching disciplinarian. He didn't waste time in reprimanding you when you had done wrong. When he chaired council meetings he was quick to call members to order during conflict and he always preached peace.'

Lebotse added: 'He converted a lot of people. He was stern. When he was really angry, he would shake. Then you knew that you were in trouble. I was like his last born so he always treated me with kid gloves. He went beyond the call of duty and invested so much of his time, effort and strength in building a community and giving us a better future.'

Mongangane is remembered as a father by all. The advice he shared and the discipline he inculcated in his children – the ones he fathered and the ones who were in his community – remain with those who still remember him.

Moremong told me: 'Ntate Mofokeng was a father in Christ. I became so close to him. I was terrified of being in the church council when he recruited me and tried to come up with excuses but at the end of the day he won me over and brought me closer to the Christian way.

'What made Ntate different from other ministers was that he was open, welcoming and fatherly. He had a loud voice, and if you were not familiar with him you'd think he shouted, but it was a habit he developed as a preacher. That loud voice ended up being his speaking voice.'

Mongangane loved his work and he was loved back by the congregation he worked for. Being one to be so involved and invested in his work, the community of Gelukspan proved to be a perfect fit. He used his talents and developed the place, taking care of the spiritual and physical health, and the educational needs, of the people.

'We never experienced any protests within the church in his time. He lived his life with dignity, and was a diligent administrator, meticulous with the finances of the church, and his private life lacked drama or scandal. He was a father figure and a true leader,' said Moremong.

* * *

In the 32 years that he was posted at Gelukspan, Mongangane served under three dominees: Ferreira, Mothobi and Marokane. While they came and went, he remained a constant factor and rooted himself deeper in the church and community life.

Moremong said: 'He encouraged slacking members to attend church and his strategy was to load them with responsibility by putting them in the church council. That seemed to work. It was either out of the respect we all had for him, or maybe to avoid the shame of having failed the church and our families.

'I remember these two Mokoena brothers that he always put on the spot to pray. The younger would say the older should pray as he was older, but he would refuse. In the end, by always picking on them, they ended up practising prayer and eventually became comfortable and rose to the occasion whenever asked to pray.'

Lebotse's face became serious and his voice rose and softened as he shared his personal story: 'As a young man working for a furniture delivery company, one day I got home and my father told me that Ntate Mofokeng had told him that the hospital was looking for staffers. I got a job working in the kitchen. I didn't like the idea of working with pots, and I thought this would make me less of a man. I asked myself how I could leave a job as a driver only to go tend to pots. I feared that I would even forget driving.

'As I contemplated quitting, Ntate Mofokeng caught wind of my plans. He gave me a written warning that if I left I would not be allowed to return. As if that wasn't enough, he came to my house to instruct me to stay put. This time he was calm and gentle. Work hard, it's going to be okay. Just don't leave the hospital, he pleaded with me. I stayed at the hospital for 30 years and it's all thanks to him. The Bophuthatswana (Bantustan) government sent me for training in Bloemfontein and I got promoted and rose through the ranks into management, all thanks to Ntate Mofokeng.'

Lebotse sees himself as part of the family.

'We grew up with Spanky, as Boy (Takatso's nickname) was already out of town to study. We played football together as brothers, and we were always together. Ntate Mofokeng was my father. He brought me up, gave me advice, reprimanded me now and then. I became a child of the Mofokeng. The only difference was our surnames, but in reality we were one people.

'Ntate Mofokeng was a beautiful soul. He was a well of wisdom and full of good advice. He knew a lot about life and shared those experiences generously. He always cautioned us against wrong. He went into evangelism fully. It was a calling. He did a lot for my family. My brother and I worked in the hospital and my children too, and he made it possible. I cannot imagine how our lives would have turned out had it not been for him.'

Moremong went dewy-eyed when he told me: 'I will always remember him as a soldier of Christ, a warrior. In EFF terms, he was a Fighter. He brought people to God. If it wasn't for him, I don't know where I would have been with my life. I appreciate that I met him while I was young and that I heard his sermons, which encouraged us.

'He was a colossal figure of his time, who commanded respect, a man of honour and humility. It is unfortunate that there is no monument or statue to show that he was there and planted the gospel. He has done enough to deserve such. When people speak of him they pay attention because his name carries so much power and influence.

'I can tell you now that if he was still around that place would not be so dilapidated and neglected. The buildings would not be flattened, he would have stood in front of the bulldozer to preserve the heritage and legacy of that place. I am convinced that he would have sourced the funds to preserve the buildings and save them from destruction. Gelukspan was a shining jewel of ingenuity and an example of a community coming together to create their own facilities led by one man and his church. It now lies in ruins.

'No man is perfect, but I cannot find anything to say about his weak points. He was strict. While other religious leaders would not shout as a form of bringing discipline, he would shout. Perhaps what counted against him would be that in tackling issues and disciplining parties at war he'd rather choose to reach a settlement and make peace, instead of getting into the issues. He applied the proverbial Elastoplast on top of the wound and would not unpack the real cause. In that way he was more reconciliatory and pushed for peace at all costs. He was a peaceful man.'

Morobe concurred: 'He was graceful and compassionate. He was soft and he disliked conflict.'

Moremong said: 'Ntate had such a sharp and great mind and a gift of memory. If life afforded us a chance to choose what we would like to inherit from our families, I'd have wished that one of his children could inherit his brain. When people talk about a brain drain, it's when we lose the likes of Ntate Mofokeng. He was a reservoir of knowledge and wisdom, a historian and a font of wisdom.'

Lebotse looked defeated as he surveyed what was left in Gelukspan. He reckoned that Mongangane's departure had meant the end of an era.

People spoke about the minister who stayed on after my grandfather retired, saying that he was a bad manager. There were confrontations between him and the congregation to the point that he was forced out of the church premises. The current minister could not find any records I could use in my research.

Lebotse said that the church lost many of its possessions in that time: the lorry and the combi because the reverend was a reckless driver, and the organ because the reverend burned it when he left.

'It's disheartening,' Lebotse said, 'that after Ntate Mofokeng left, the church lost its belongings. We have not known peace since then. A lot of people scattered in different directions. Some left and joined the church in Itsoseng township.

'When we lost the elders like Ntate, we took many steps backwards.'

11
The 'luck' in Gelukspan

I return to Takatso to reflect on the family legacy and what's to salvage from the ruins of Gelukspan.

It is evident that, as the hospital grew in stature and size, it became a big employer in the area and provided livelihoods. But the growth spurt didn't necessarily make the Mofokeng family wealthy. On the contrary, when the shovels were put down and the dignitaries cut the ribbon to open the facilities, Mongangane was in the crowds and not on the podium. He never received any glory. His name was not included in the memorial stone of the church, nor does the hospital bear his name anywhere. This never bothered him, because his was salt-of-the-earth goodness and he didn't seek external praise or validation. It was from the goodwill of the church people and the community that he would find his grace.

Takatso said: 'We got to Gelukspan with nothing to our name but a few items. A church elder named Ntate Twala who lived on the other side of Mafeking gave us a cow, and a push for my father to get into cattle farming. He sent us the cow with a calf so that we could have a supply of milk. After the calf was grown its mother went back to the Twalas while it stayed with us. It was *kgomo ya mafisa* (a borrowed cow) that was milked by Spanky and my father. I was my mother's son while Spanky was my father's, and he looked after the cows. We have never forgotten the generosity and kindness of Ntate Twala.'

More benevolence was to come when the community offered

the Mofokengs a piece of land to cultivate, some five morgen, which was ploughed by a family friend and congregant Ntate Morobe along with his son Mabuti, and by Takatso. The land yielded a decent harvest of mealies, sunflowers and pumpkins in a good year.

Takatso said at that time they experienced the warmth and *botho (ubuntu)* of Batswana.

'The people were giving. During the summer harvest we would have a beeline of benefactors dropping off watermelons, mealies and pumpkins, when they came over to the hospital or even in transit to town in Mafeking or Lichtenburg.

'We were brought up in the Setswana ways with all the other children. During the ploughing season I would team up with Mabuti of the Morobe family. We spanned oxen and lined them up, and tilled his ten morgen first, and then we moved over to my family's five morgen. There were no tractors then.

'The first people to own a tractor in Gelukspan were the Ramothibe family and they became so rich. I remember when I finished matric, I was the very first child in the whole of the Reserve to complete matric, and Ntate Ramothibe visited us at home. On his way out he told me that he heard that I finished matric and invited me to come drive his tractor for him. I politely declined and told him that I was going to further my studies. I never forget that I, as the first matriculant in the whole of Lichtenburg Reserve, was offered to drive Ntate Ramothibe's tractor as my achievement and reward.'

Takatso said even though Gelukspan had become home, he was never really fully happy that his father lived among Batswana. 'I felt like they had trapped my father against his will. But he never wanted to go back to his people. His idea of missionary work was about developing people and looking after them, and not his own people, but people in faraway lands. He became a Morolong and was welcomed and revered among the Barolong.

'My father was physically strong. Not even riding a scooter and being exposed to the elements that could bring him harm could weaken him. Some people have to deal with the effects of spending too much time on motorbikes, but not my father.'

* * *

Takatso has come a long way since the offer by Ntate Ramothibe to drive his tractor as the first matriculant in Gelukspan. He went as far as earning a PhD in theology from the Ivy League Princeton University in the US.

He said there was no other option.

'We came to Gelukspan with nothing and our fortunes were changed by education. Our hope was to keep education in the family, and indeed we stuck to school. When I finished Standard 6, others stayed to drive tractors and I went to boarding school in Emmarentia. I travelled by bus with Hilda Lebotse (who married Ezekiel) as we went to further our education. My parents sacrificed everything to ensure that we went to school because we didn't have anything else. It helped that we were intelligent.'

After his BA degree at Turfloop (now University of Limpopo), he studied in the Netherlands and eventually the United States of America.

'When I got to Princeton University, as part of our training, there was an evening where an African American was invited to conscientise us about the issues of social ills we could face in America. He did a big job that man. He asked us to close our eyes and think back to when we first saw a White person. I went back to Orlando Shelters and remembered the White boy and White girl who played the guitar in the street. I also remembered the White guard in the train to Springs when we went to visit my aunt.

Then in Gelukspan, for a stretch of land over 100 kilometres from the east to the west and over 60 kilometres from the north to the south, I only knew of three White men, so White people didn't mean anything to us.'

* * *

It wasn't until Takatso got to Emmarentia that he felt White power and presence.

He became involved in student activism in 1961, a few weeks after the first commemoration of the Sharpeville Massacre, and after South Africa became a republic. He was expelled for his political activities and had to return to Gelukspan, breaking the hearts of his parents.

'I felt like I had shamed the family and the community, so much so that my father asked me to spend more time indoors than outside because people were beginning to ask why I wasn't at school.

'Emmarentia refused to release my books, and told me I wouldn't be allowed to write my exams in Transvaal. So I went to seek refuge at Barolong High School in Mafeking, which was under the Cape Province. The principal there, Mr CN Lekalake, was understanding when I told him my story. I was very proud of what I did in Emmarentia and he allowed me space. So I went back home and studied by myself for six months and when the results came, I was the only one who passed that year. All their candidates at Barolong High School had failed.'

The Mofokeng's journey was crowned by Takatso's success. The family had arrived in Gelukspan in 1952 with very little, into a community that they did not know but grew to be a part of. Takatso's father – and Takatso himself, as a *dagaboy* – took part in the building of the church and the hospital, using their own hands and the strength of their backs to allow buildings that would serve thousands of people for decades to arise on the flat land.

Takatso became the first matriculant in the Trust, earning the offer to drive Ramothibe's tractor. Instead, he went on to Emmarentia to study, where he fell from grace as an activist against oppression. He redeemed himself spectacularly at Barolong High School and went on to study at what is considered one of the finest educational institutions in the world.

Takatso stands as proof that the Gelukspan mission, headed by the indomitable patriarch Mongangane, was worthwhile.

What Takatso is modest enough not to tell me is that, in one generation, out of the desolation and hopelessness of being a Black South African during apartheid, he became the first in his family and extended clan to return from the USA as an Ivy League graduate. His grandfather had worked on the farms of the Free State, his father was a mission-school-educated community builder, and he had scaled the heights of education, earning a PhD and going on to carve a career for himself as a respected Black theologian.

Perhaps that was the 'luck' in Gelukspan.

12

Family reflections

Grandad Mongangane and the author. PHOTO: ELIZABETH SEJAKE

I travelled to the small eastern Free State town of Lindley to see my other uncle, Tsietsi Chapatso. Tsietsi is Mongangane's nephew and the brother of my grandfather's adopted daughter Tshidiso. He lived in the household of Mongangane and possesses first-hand knowledge of life back then.

I pull up to the house in Tsekeletsa Street in Ntha township, across the road from Lindley, just before noon. Tsietsi is a man of influence. He has lived into his eighties and his wisdom on matters of the family and tradition is unmatched. He is a former mayor of

Ntha and a prominent figure at the local Uniting Reformed Church, and remains a revered member of the community. In fact, when the small township got new roads, the plan was to name one of the main streets after him, an honour, he tells me, he just could not bring himself to accept. He plays the horses and says he has mastered the art of betting.

He leads me to one of the backrooms where a musty smell of sheep hide permeates the air. He is busy softening the hide with his bare wrinkly hands as he gently rubs it like he was washing it. He tells me that some of his grandchildren (nephews I have never met) would be returning from the mountain after weeks of initiation.

We settle down for a talk. All the while, he is working the leather.

Mongangane was his father Takatso's best bet for a better life for the family, and it paid off, Tsietsi tells me. Mongangane never worked a day on the farm and with the education he received from Thaba Nchu he could become something else other than a farm labourer.

Tsietsi's version of how Mongangane converted his mother to Christianity was different to the one I had come to know. According to him, Selloane was never converted. He says it wasn't until she died that Mongangane threw his mother's traditional tools in the river Thethana.

'It's not easy to understand,' he says. 'When you are no longer physically strong you can never work as a sangoma. It takes a lot to heal people and administer medicines and the like. There was not much Selloane could do with the tools of her trade because there was no one willing to step up and inherit them. Most of the family was being converted to Christianity. So Mongangane saw no use for them and as such disposed of them. Towards the end of her life, Selloane went to her family in Senekal where she died.'

As much as Mongangane had accepted Christianity, Tsietsi maintains that he didn't completely cut his links with tradition. He had a traditional healer that he consulted whenever he came home as a young man, as is customary of Basotho.

'His doctor, who was called Lekula la Matlere, used to strengthen him and then he would return to his life in Johannesburg having being cleansed and having received the blessings from the ancestors. You can't just carry on with life without observing your traditional rituals, otherwise you will die. It's suicidal and self-defeating to not cleanse and get strengthened by your family,' Tsietsi explains.

My elder cousin's brother Rasebopela, who lived with Mongangane for most of his childhood, believes Mongangane set himself on a Christian path and only honoured tradition on certain occasions, such as death and funeral rituals that he practiced as part of the mourning process. He reminds me of the incident when Mongangane attempted a traditional thanksgiving ceremony and nine of his grandchildren narrowly escaped a motor accident on their way home. Rasebopela says this put Mongangane off any desire to practice traditional rituals, except for mourning purposes.

I believe that the incidents mentioned by Tsietsi must have happened in the earlier days of Mongangane's evangelistic life. In my memory of him, he was vehemently opposed to the practice of traditional healers and sangomas. He was vocal about how he didn't believe in them. Instead he held on to the gospel and his faith to overcome adversity.

Tsietsi says in a competitive world where there are winners and losers, one needs to be rooted in one's traditions.

My Uncle Takatso, Mongangane's second son, has also reflected on the reality that his father may have needed more than a prayer to get him by.

'Christianity alienated us from our traditions and this manifested in many ways, including the fact that we didn't go to the mountain where culture is transmitted to younger men. So we missed out on that opportunity to be groomed into traditional Sotho men,' Takatso told me.

Tsietsi, when I saw him, agreed: 'Mongangane lost his Bosotho, because he didn't take his children to initiation. That was a mistake. Most of the family members have shunned tradition and have chosen religion.

'I am still steadfast in tradition. I will practise it to the end. If my children choose not to practise it, it would be their choice, but the Bible says Abraham was instructed by God to take all his sons to the mountain so that they could be the chosen people. He further said I want to be your God and for you to be my people even the ones you bought with money, you must initiate. Now if you don't initiate your sons, how will they be God's chosen people?

'We were fearful of the church. People could not practise their traditions. I told my church and my minister that I would continue to practise my tradition, my wife would remain a sangoma, and that all my sons would be initiated,' Tsietsi said.

In spite of his strong opinions on tradition versus the call of Christianity, he argued that the choice Mongangane made to go with religion over tradition did not break the family apart.

'We accepted it and worked harmoniously with him. He was the only one who opted out of tradition.'

Tsietsi told the story that Mongangane once, on a visit home, told him that he had taken one of his older grandsons to be circumcised, and that he'd decided to take his grandsons to hospital for the procedure rather than to let them go to the mountain.

The disadvantage of this, Tsietsi said, was that people who had gone to the mountain looked down on those who'd gone the medical route and had been 'cut by women'. He said 'you must do everything your kinsmen did in the mountain' or 'you will not know the secret codes of the pack'.

Takatso, on the other hand, has memories of how Mongangane didn't completely shun tradition. He believes that his father showed allegiance to tradition even when in service of the church. He recalls an incident when Mongangane had to go to court for a matter that involved the licence of his scooter that had expired. He needed protection from the wrath of the authorities, so he woke up early in the morning to cut *lekgala* (aloe) into a basin full of water and then bathed in it.

Aloe occupies a place of reverence among Basotho. It is used in cleansing ceremonies. It is believed to remove bad luck and bad omens. Takatso doesn't say whether the court case was decided in Mongangane's favour or not.

In his later years Mongangane undoubtedly played the important role of the community elder. It was at his feet that younger Basotho men learnt about traditional practices and conventions. He would advise them on how to properly mourn in the Sesotho ways, and he knew how the meat was to be shared among men, women, boys and girls. He could also guide people in the brewing of traditional beer. Clearly the upbringing in Riga, where he had been born, stayed with him for life even in his guise as a modern African.

That Mongangane dabbled in the two worlds of tradition and religion is clear in Takatso's head. In North West he was, in the eyes of his congregation, as close to being a saint as it was possible to be, but when he crossed the Vaal river into the Free State he was Mongangane, the traditionalist.

Takatso reminded me that as a missionary trained at the Stofberg-Gedenkskool, Mongangane had to put on the hat of a policeman and toe the line of Western Christianity. As such he would be a different character depending on which side of the Vaal he found himself on.

He was a strict adherent of the Western Christian faith. He prayed daily, and his sermons shook mountains and moved congregants to tears. But he never abandoned what made him a Mosotho man.

Takatso told me he had conversations with Mongangane closer to the end his life and these were revealing about his thoughts on the afterlife.

Mongangane's father had died at 54; Mongangane himself at 94. When Takatso asked him his thoughts about the fact that his father had died a much younger man, and whether he thought he would meet him again after death, his response was that his father would still be getting older where he was.

'I asked him where he would be going. He told me that he would be with his father, his mother, my mother and his sons. That was an interesting response given that Western Christianity only speaks of meeting the disciples and Jesus in the afterlife. It doesn't include your immediate family, but these strangers from the Bible that you've never met and chances are that they don't know you either. So for him to choose his family shows that he believed that the ancestors would be there to welcome him,' Takatso said.

Mongangane played his role as an elder in the Mofokeng family. As his father had expected, he had looked after his nephews and nieces.

Tsietsi remembers how in 1943, when they were left as orphans in Skuilplaas, Mongangane asked for them to stay with the Ntsala family where Mongangane's sister Madibuseng was married. The elder nephew, known as Boy Boy, left with some cows and a horse, while the young Tsietsi was transported on a bicycle by Mongangane until they reached his new home.

'Then he left for Johannesburg and used to come as often as he could to check up on us, like a father would.'

By 1953, one of the Ntsala sons went for initiation in Matsheleng and Tsietsi was left behind to herd and milk the cows in the White man's *huis*. He dropped out of school in 1955, and went to be initiated the following year.

He got married and left Matsheleng in 1965, moving to Lindley, where he has lived ever since. Taking a cue from his uncle Mongangane, Tsietsi says he used to check up on his other cousins and, when they died, he buried them.

Tsietsi remembers Mongangane for the pearls of wisdom he shared with his nephew.

'He used to tell me that one had to protect oneself here on earth. Don't have expectations for people. Stand on your own because nobody owes you favours."

A pain that defined the Mofokeng family in the 1970s was the death of Damara Chapatso, a promising soccer star who lived in Welkom in the Free State. His father, Lekgowa, was Mongangane's cousin. Damara was a star in demand. Everybody loved him and he was wanted by teams in Welkom and Bloemfontein. He was killed by a friend.

Tsietsi said this was a realisation that people didn't wish others well and also that soccer was no good and he put education over everything else. This echoes to some degree Mongangane's wisdoms: to protect oneself, to stand on your own two feet because no one owed you anything.

After all this time, Tsietsi still holds Mongangane in high regard.

'He taught me to take care of myself. He told me everything I needed to know about our forefathers. I have the memory he left me with. He was a man of peace and was never into funny businesses. He spoke out when you lost the plot and he taught us to love family.'

As we parted, Tsietsi urged me to never lose connection with the ancestors.

'People don't take our traditions and customs seriously. They dismiss them, but the truth is that they work and they have an impact on our lives. You must walk with your *badimo* (ancestors) wherever you go. Whatever you do or ask for, call on them to plead for you to the Almighty then you will prosper. We pray to the God of our forefathers, our grandfathers and grandmothers. Don't leave the roots of your family tree. You are a branch of it. Always call on your ancestors.'

This conversation reminded me of what Robin Wells concedes. He says: 'Christianity has undoubtedly alienated large numbers of Basotho from valuable aspects of their own cultural heritage'. Christianity produced a new means of expression and frameworks to define one's identity.

It has become a common occurrence in today's churches to see a traditional healer wearing beads and animal skins put on their church uniform and attend a service. Balancing African traditional practices and Christian persuasions often attracts stares of judgment among the converted. But with the rise of traditional healers and sangomas Africans are responding to their ancestors' call, while carrying the Bible in the other hand.

13

The wind beneath his wings

Mahadi Mofokeng, in the middle holding the clock, with cat-eye spectacles, was a leader of the Christelike Vroue Vereeniging (CVV). Next to her on the right is Mantlaletseng Morobe, who was interviewed for this book.
PHOTO: FAMILY ALBUM

When the jacarandas bloom in Joburg in October and drop their pretty purple petals to create a magnificent carpet, I always think of the jacarandas we used to climb at home in Lotlhakane village. These are happy memories.

Lotlhakane is a sprawling village some 15 kilometres south of the centre of Mahikeng town and some 30 kilometres north of Gelukspan. This is the place that became our family home when my grandparents retired from their missionary work. It's the place where the bones of the patriarch and matriarch lie among the Barolong, who were not, originally, their people. The Barolong booRapulana first settled here in 1777.

Dr Andrew Smith, the Scottish-born explorer who travelled across South Africa in the early 19th century and recorded the flora and fauna he encountered in his missions, provided a rare glimpse into history and what life was like for our ancestors. His expedition, which lasted 18 months, took him to Basutoland where he met Moshoeshoe at his fortress of Thaba Bosiu. He also reached Kuruman and the Magaliesberg.

Smith wrote of Lotlhakane of the 1830s in the diary he kept during the Expedition for Exploring Central Africa. He said it was a place rich with animal life and describes a Bushman lark that he met on the grass flats near the village. He mentions a 'takhaitsi' – some sort of antelope – that, when approached closely, immediately lay down in the grass and remained there, standing up only at the last minute to assert itself. He documents a blue wildebeest with a 'logwood' coloured belly.

Close to 200 years later, Lotlhakane teems with human life more than animals, save for a few cattle, goats, sheep, donkeys and horses. It is stripped of any signs of the resilient wildlife that roamed these plains. You may, however, spot a rabbit or some buck in the wild thorn bush outside the village, sometimes a scavenger out to terrorise sheep or goats kept in *moraka* (a place outside a residential area where people keep their flock). The village has modern features like electricity, but most of the roads remain untarred and the river with reeds is mostly dry. Lotlhakane gets its name from the *matlhaka* (reeds) of this river.

* * *

Lotlhakane is scorching in summer and freezing in winters – normal weather for the semi-arid savannah that is the Kalahari. It is a typical Setswana village in North West province steeped in tradition under the leadership of Kgosi Tebogo Seatlholo, who was elected in 2022 as the chairperson of the National House of Traditional and Khoisan Leaders (NHTKL).

But it is also a place reached by modernity. Amapiano by Kabza De Small and Maphorisa, Makhadzi and Master KG, Motswako (Setswana hip-hop) by Khuli Chana, Tuks Senganga, Notshi and traditional music by Mmaausi boom from the many taverns, shebeens and clubs of the village, with revellers kicking up dust to their latest hits. On special Sundays they host jazz sessions with some famous DJs from Motsweding FM making a celebrity appearance. It is flat and dusty, often sleepy, but it has its moments of vibrancy.

* * *

These days the blooming jacarandas are a reminder of my loss. My grandmother, Mahadi Mofokeng, passed away on 2 October 2005 with the jacarandas all over the Highveld in full bloom. She was 86 when she died in Thusong Hospital near Itsoseng township. She died on the eve of an operation to amputate her foot due to diabetes complications. My grandfather, then 91, survived her and my aunt Tshidiso and I cared for him.

I have added the season of the blooming trees to my calendar. It is a reminder of my loss and my tears, but it is also a beautiful time to celebrate the life of a woman who gave me so much.

My grandmother, Mahadi Maria Mofokeng (born Chaane), was not an inconsequential bystander in the life of her powerful husband Mongangane. If a man is the head of the family, then the woman is indeed the neck that directs the actions of the head.

This was certainly true of her. She was no pushover and never one to cower and submit. The story of her entrepreneurial spirit and homemaking skills is of great interest to me and reveals a bit more about the pecking order in the Mofokeng household and its daily business.

The Oxford Dictionary describes a housewife (also known as a homemaker) as a woman whose main occupation is managing household affairs and doing housework. In addition, she cares for her children, and is in charge of buying, cooking and storing food for the family. In the traditional definition, she is a person who is not employed outside the home.

Mahadi was a textbook version of a housewife, but her managerial skills extended beyond the walls of the home she made with Mongangane.

* * *

She was the de facto mother of the Gelukspan Hospital complex. She was called Mme with affection and sincerity by everybody inside the church and out. It was largely due to Mahadi's warmth and generosity that the mission house in which the family lived became a refuge for many in desperate situations, for destitute families, and those who had simply missed the last bus home after visiting the hospital. She laid out the beds and offered a warm meal to guests, as well as a sympathetic, caring ear for their troubles.

Mahadi's go-getter spirit shone through when she whipped out her Singer sewing machine to become the local tailor and dressmaker, skilfully crafting the black woollen hats, white collars and black jackets for the Christelike Vroue Vereeniging (CVV), which was, and still is, the women's ministry of the NG Kerk, and the luxurious black velvet hats for the women in Mokgatlo wa Bacha

BaBakreste, the church's youth ministry. As the evangelist's wife, it was her responsibility to clothe the new members at the special Good Friday service, and the newly clothed would wear their new outfits with pride when attending church services in their local branches.

She also worked in the Tlamelang Special School. She would tell us stories of how the carers kicked off their blankets at 4 am, so that when the children living with disabilities got up they would have warm water to bath, and their breakfast would be ready. She and the other carers would make their beds and then wheel them to different sections of the hospital for assessment, physiotherapy, classes or some time outdoors in the sun. I suppose that earned her bragging rights to be known as a nurse.

It was during one of the shifts that she slipped and landed on her knee. An X-ray investigation showed that she had not fractured it, but the knee never recovered. Whenever the sharp pain tore through her knee unexpectedly, she always wondered whether she'd been misdiagnosed. Not that it slowed her down, she put on a elasticated knee brace to get around and function. She carried heavy loads and buckets of water, always on the move, always fixing something, always cleaning. She was never one to sit on her hands.

Mahadi always reminded me that she was the first patient to get a set of false teeth when the dental clinic opened at the hospital. They lasted decades because of her diligent care and attention. She would frighten us as children when she took them out and exposed her bottom naked gums like a magician. It was freaky and we would gasp in shock.

Takatso encapsulated the spirit of Mahadi when he called her a 'self-made food technologist'. Mahadi became a one-woman home-industry with her tenacity and her never-say-die enterprising spirit.

She earned her own legendary reputation as the resident baker in Gelukspan, making the most appetising buns that side of the Western Transvaal.

The smell of freshly baked goods in the oven wafted out of the Mofokeng home into the nearby houses, attracting many eager customers who were also taken by their golden brown colour and the cushy soft inside, not to mention her secret ingredients that gave a kick in the mouth. The buns came in plain and raisin variety too. She would extend the life of her bakes by turning them into rusks. She devised some way of using the oven at a particular heat to speed up the drying process without burning the rusks. She really was a food technologist. Once they had dried, she would store them and they would be dipped in tea for months to come.

It was only in conversation with my aunt Tshidiso in recent times that I learn that Mahadi had used her sister Masabata Sefatsa's mother-in-law's bun recipe. The family had been visiting in Kroonstad, Orange Free State where she saw the Sefatsa matriarch make what was called *mabaso*. This so intrigued Mahadi that she asked for the recipe and replicated it in Gelukspan adding her own twist and some flavour here and there. She extended the recipe to turn it into *magwinya* (also known by its Afrikaans name 'vetkoek') that sold like, well, hot cakes. Tshidiso herself interned in the kitchen as an assistant to Mahadi and witnessed the magic first hand.

Tshidiso said the success of the buns business was nothing short of a phenomenon for a housewife. With the money she made, Mahadi managed to buy furniture at Gremm's Furnishers in Lichtenburg, including a kitchen suite, cupboards, sofas and beds, all delivered to her busy home in Gelukspan.

* * *

Mongangane, Mahadi and the author in Gelukspan in front of the family peach tree in 1984. PHOTO: TAKATSO MOFOKENG

Ever industrious, Mahadi spent time outside in the garden tending to her vegetable patch. She grew mealies, flat white boer pumpkins, sunflowers, spinach, beans, onions, tomatoes, carrots, cabbages and beetroot. Her 'farming' was small scale, but the harvest was enough to share with neighbours.

A good year with the peach trees would yield hundreds of the yellow cling and dessert variety as well as what was known as *lospit* – literally meaning 'loose pip' – which were popular for being soft and mushy without losing the texture and sweetness of a good peach.

Mahadi would preserve the peaches, cutting them in halves or quarters and then creating a thick syrup by boiling white sugar and water. The peaches would be placed in a Consol glass jar and the hot syrup poured in to capacity. The most crucial stage of the preservation process was the closure of the jar with a stainless steel lid. I remember that this had to be executed swiftly and with precision; one mistake and the oxygen quotient exceeded what was required, the contents would begin to ferment within days and have to be thrown out as waste.

After the bottling, the jars would then be covered in layers of thick cloth to maintain warmth for at least a day and our year's supply of canned fruit would fill the cupboards in the pantry. Custard and peaches or bread pudding with peaches became a Sunday lunch dessert staple at home. She could package these jars and give some of the bounty to neighbours, friends and family with a stern warning that the jars had to be returned before the next peach season.

Ever the enterprising homemaker, she expanded her preserves to include tomato relish and jam made out of peaches, apricots or mulberries. She managed to pass this skill on to her daughters-in-law who continue to practise this family tradition.

She continued to produce *mangangajane* (dried peaches) like she had done in Stofberg. Much like Takatso and Spanky, who in 1949 climbed to the rafters to steal the peaches, I have vivid memories from the 1980s of us, the grandchildren, helping ourselves to the drying fruit. If it wasn't our sticky little fingers thinning out the supplies, it was the pesky little birds that descended to ravage the peaches. Fortunately for us, the years had made Mahadi softer and she didn't unleash her wrath on us like she did on our fathers. Whatever she could salvage in the end of the drying period would be our year's supply of sweet nibbles. Some of the peaches were turned into stewed fruit for dessert or breakfast to go with yoghurt. *Motoho* (soft porridge) is a breakfast staple in Basotho homes. It comes in the soured variety, known as *seqaqabola* or plain, called *lesheleshele*. The soured flavour has its roots in the traditional beer-brewing culture, using *tomoso* (a yeast-like agent). While she never brewed beer, or drank it, Mahadi was an expert at brewing *seqaqabola* either with *mabele* (sorghum) or with mealie meal. She would also extend its life by turning it into *mahleu* (mageu) that she served her guests as an alternative drink to tea or coffee. It took a skill of its own to ensure that the *mahleu* was smooth and not lumpy, and this was in the stirring of the pot and the time on the stove. This filling drink was served cold in summer and hot in winter.

Of all the animals that 'agreed' with her, the chickens seemed to be her biggest passion. There were turkeys and ducks in the yard, but they were side shows. The stars were the chickens. She would have over 100 milling the yard, big and small, black, white, yellow and grey. She had the patience to raise little one-day old chicks until they were old enough to fend for themselves. Even in retirement, the chicken remained her spirit animal. They would gather around her, sit on her and, like a mother hen, she would marshal the flock to their enclosure where she would feed them crushed maize or whole corn depending on their age.

* * *

Mahadi believed in the adage 'cleanliness is next to godliness'. She was obsessed with sparkling, airy spaces. Her kitchen was always neat and spotless, the dishes washed and packed away. She obsessed about the kitchen cloth that wiped the cupboards and other surfaces. She preferred them to be white so that she could quickly spot the stained ones and relegate them without delay to the shame of being a *skroplap* (rags for washing or wiping the floor).

She loved her linen white, because she believed that angels visited us in our sleep in the night and that it was fitting that they found us sleeping in the colour of purity, cleanliness and godliness.

She took pride in the beauty of her surroundings and always decorated her house with pride, especially the *voorhuis* (sitting room), pairing a new set of floral curtains with an arrangement of flowers from the garden. Little artefacts picked up on trips to the Orange Free State, to Durban or to Botswana would be installed in the living room with pride. She may have had western inclinations, but her African aesthetic always revealed itself.

With a lifelong appreciation of choral music, she loved curling up on the sofa with her *Hosanna* hymnbook, going through the staff notation as she practised a new hymn. Her depth and knowledge of the hymns of the NG Kerk was unmatched. This love for music can be traced back to her earlier years as the daughter of *ou* Chaane, a pastor of the Apostolic Faith Mission church, which she amusingly pronounced as 'Five Mission'. She'd grown up singing Sesotho hymns from the iconic *Lifela tsa Sione* hymn book. The *Hosanna* took a substantial number of hymns from *Lifela tsa Sione*. She always occupied a place in the soprano section of the church choir while my grandfather would be in baritone. They earned a plethora of trophies at regional church choir competitions under the baton of Mistress Dorothy Morapedi.

Mahadi loved God. She prayed. She once told me that she preferred praying to preaching as she connected better with the higher power in a state of prayer.

* * *

Shopping – the mail order kind – brought Mahadi so much joy. She introduced me to the wondrous world of Charles Velkes, a retailer of goods including crockery, cutlery, electrical equipment, clothing, ornaments and decorative items. The company was ahead of its time in a certain way: just like today's lockdown and quarantine businesses, it had no showroom or premises. Instead, it sent out catalogues to customers at intervals throughout the year. The customers then sent their orders to an address in Cape Town and the goods would be delivered by post. In the Seventies and Eighties, the company was riding high. Only about 40 per cent of its customers lived in South Africa. The rest were spread across Botswana, Swaziland, Transkei, Bophuthatswana and South West Africa.

When the catalogue arrived, she would ogle the colourful pictures, read the brief description and scan the price. At the back of the book was a perforated order form, which she would carefully tear out, fill in and put in an envelope. Then she would send us to the post office in the hospital complex. Payment either had to accompany the order or be made on delivery.

Collecting her packages from PO Box 1, Radithuso – our postal address – rivalled Christmas festivities. The oohs, the ahs and the gasps of delight when she discovered that the ornament she'd ordered actually looked better in real life than in the catalogue were too precious. She would waste no time placing an order for a second batch of goodies.

My grandmother was a skilled bargain hunter. We did most of our grocery shopping around the Lucky 7 specials cycle. The local general dealer, owned by Shepstone Molamu, would issue the catalogue of the goodies on sale. Mahadi would sit down with a pen and mark what she needed and the quantity she needed it in. We would then be sent off with boxes to collect the grocery. The Lucky 7 sign became synonymous with her. Even in retirement, she looked out for the shop that carried the Lucky 7 specials and lo and behold, Shadi's General Dealer in Lotlhakane did. My assignment was never to miss the catalogue and I would rush home to show her the mind blowing special of 2.5 kg of flour at a shockingly low price R1.29 from the R2.50 it was in store.

Mahadi's favourite flower was a rose. White roses, specifically because, well, white is pure and clean, and Rose happened to be her mother's second name. So wherever she lived, she grew a little patch of roses. Even the hard and unforgiving soil of Mafeking had to be tilled and fertilised until at least two bushes bore some petals to brighten an old lady's days.

* * *

She loved education. She always said that if she had been born at a different time she would have gone on to earn a doctorate, but life and the universe conspired that she would go only as far as Standard 3. But seeing how she wrote her letters in cursive, and considering her command of language, it is clear that she didn't stop bettering herself beyond school. She was more than just literate; she was educated straight from the university of life.

As tradition dictated, Mahadi was Mrs Mofokeng, but she didn't lose her birth totem, a lion. She was *moradi wa Chaane* (the daughter of Chaane), a Motaung (a person of the lion). You would never want to get on her wrong side. She could roar when she was angry, and she was a strict disciplinarian who spoke her mind. She had a sharp wit and a great sense of humour. A Mosotho woman who shot from the hip, she was never dishonest or deceptive. Sometimes her directness made me uncomfortable, because words in one language might carry a different meaning in another. There were words she would say and I would cringe, because they sounded like swear words, but to her Sotho ear she was being explicit enough to be understood and for her words never to be misconstrued.

She was irrepressible, indomitable, sophisticated and classy.

It was on her back that the family of Mofokeng was raised and rested.

14

The Rollands of Beersheba

There is a page missing in the chapters of South African history. A part overlooked, forgotten and not spoken about as often as it should be. Somehow, when the great bloody episodes of South African wars are remembered, no mention is made of the Beersheba Massacre of Black Christians.

This is a little-known episode.

The thriving mission station of Beersheba in the eastern Free State, founded by Samuel Rolland, was annihilated by marauding Boer trekkers. The event has been a subject of debate in small academic circles but had never been part of a larger conversation about religion, bloodshed and the destruction Boers left in their wake as they trekked inland.

A standing church and a community of MaRoellane, entrenched in the traditions of SeRoellane, was razed to the ground and its remnants appropriated into the Boer church.

* * *

Samuel Rolland of the Paris Evangelical Missionary Society was a powerful figure in Beersheba and the surrounding eastern Free State settlements and was a representative of Moshoeshoe who had appointed him to supervise the area.

Moshoeshoe had indicated to Sir George Napier of the British government in the Cape Colony that the land inhabited by Basotho included the entire area between the Senqu (Orange) river in the south and Lekoa (Vaal) river in the north. The Maluti in the east marked the boundary between the Basotho and the AmaZulu. The boundary in the west was the meeting point of the two rivers mentioned above. The British government in the Cape colony recognised those boundaries. The land west of the meeting point of those rivers was inhabited by Batlhaping.

The first White people to cross the Senqu from the Cape Colony were hunters and traders. They first met Basotho and sought permission to trade and hunt from Moshoeshoe and the chiefs of the area where they were to engage in their trade and animal hunting. These same hunters and traders are the people who passed on information about the land, its fertility, its people and its form of government.

When the Boers in the Cape Colony realised that there was more grass for grazing north of the Senqu, they wished to take their cattle there. The entire area was populated by Basotho who had villages governed by chiefs who acknowledged Moshoeshoe as the king. These were small farmers who ploughed, kept animals and hunted. When Henry Douglas Warden – who was known as Major Warden and who represented British interests north of the Senqu – insisted on setting up recognisable boundaries between the area occupied by White farmers and Basotho, Moshoeshoe, in a letter written to the missionary Rolland who had established a thriving mission station called Beersheba, listed conditions for the area.

When individual Boers arrived, they had to get permission from Moshoeshoe. They also knew that they had to seek permission from the deputy governor in the Cape Colony. Andries Stockenström gave them that permission on certain conditions, which had been negotiated with Moshoeshoe. Those conditions included that the Boers should return to the Cape Colony at the end of a three-months' stay in the land of Basotho. They were not allowed to erect any buildings nor could they till the land.

The weakness of this arrangement was that it was not written and was not monitored and policed by either of the two authorities. It's success depended on the willingness of the individual Boers to adhere to the agreement.

All historians of the time say that the temptation to transgress lay in the power of the Boers that derived from owning guns. The foreigners gradually and deliberately transgressed as soon as their numbers increased and the numbers of their guns increased. Basotho did not have guns to enforce the terms.

* * *

Samuel and Elizabeth Rolland had established a mission station at Beersheba that soon thrived. In her account of their life and work there, Elizabeth writes that her husband took excursions and frequently returned with small parties of natives who were willing to be placed at Beersheba under their care.

Elizabeth opened an infant school, which she described as *lelapa*: 'nothing better than an open space enclosed by tall reeds'. Later, Elizabeth called on a liberated slave, whom she identifies as Aaron, to build her a schoolroom that could accommodate 200 children.

The children made rapid progress and could read the Sesotho/Setswana Bible.

A group of Batlharo moved into Beersheba too in the winter of 1835, and the building of a new town began in earnest, with the construction of hive-like huts that formed a circle. The huts were the same size and the thatching was done with 'extreme neatness', the doors and windows were coloured with various earth tones giving it a pretty and artistic appearance.

'Public balls took place in the enclosure, there were dances to propitiate the rain clouds, softer tones and slower movements for the recovery of the sick, hoarse war-cry and masculine roar to frighten the enemy, and the dead and wounded were lamented with melancholy howling. Initiations balls lasted several nights,' Elizabeth reminisced.

The larger hut, which was used as a school building, became the church and it could seat 200 converts.

The missionary's hut was open until well into the night. Elizabeth records that wandering farmers who visited the lonely missionary station often warned them they could not live in such a barren place. Swarms of locusts sometimes devastated the vegetation and droughts sometimes decimated the crops. Inhabitants confronted famine along with their missionary leaders. But Samuel 'continued in faith and prayer'.

The Rollands moved into a more comfortable home of four rooms and a kitchen built by an English mason. They cultivated a garden, including a vineyard, in front of the house after they dug out hard pot clay and brought in new soil in from other places for the seeds to thrive.

* * *

The large school house, which served as a church, was where early Basotho converts congregated. They planted reeds in the form of a large cross and covered them with wattle and daub, and then with grass used for thatching. Seats and pulpit were made out of unburnt bricks and white clay was smeared on the lower parts of the walls.

Elizabeth writes that Samuel would, at sunrise, gather all the young shepherds to read and sing. The school bell was a French horn that reverberated over the valleys to summon the inhabitants. Infants were separated from their mothers and were looked after by Elizabeth, while Samuel taught old and young men and women. Some 20 years after they had settled there, there was a change in climate: locusts became rare and rains were regular. The number of converts increased by hundreds too.

'The blessing of the Lord fell in rich grace on the labours of His faithful servant,' Elizabeth wrote about her husband.

Samuel continued his missionary work and brought in more converts. Basotho returning to the kingdom from across the Colonies stopped over at Beersheba. Some were already members of churches. They presented their certificates to Samuel. This resulted in a spike in the number of inhabitants.

Church was held for the converts and sometimes the unconverted joined. Elizabeth writes that men came in filthy sheepskins hanging down their backs and women wore nothing more than a string of beads round their loins from which hung a kind of apron ornamented with beads or buttons. Both men and women were smeared with fat and red ochre. There were voices of dissent in the church, with some yelling while Samuel preached: 'Do you still listen to the lies he is telling?' Or: 'That's enough, let us go home.'

I found it fascinating to read the writings of Elizabeth Rolland, which are not readily accessible to the general public. They are essential for understanding early Christianity in South Africa. The sermons were not readily welcome. There were murmurs of resistance towards the foreign religion. And yet the missionaries showed dogged determination. They pushed on with the gospel, no matter what adversity came their way.

Samuel was set on teaching his converts, and potential converts, to sing but Elizabeth said he was met with silence as he sought to lead them to imitate the simplest harmonies. He kept at it because he believed that singing hymns was one of the most powerful means for training the mind.

First to sing along were the youngsters. Samuel played the flute, cornet, violin and the piano. He identified a few good voices that he used in public worship and so slowly improved participation.

* * *

At the first French missionary conference hosted in Beersheba in 1836, missionaries Eugene Casalis, Thomas Arbousset, Constant Goselin, Francois Daumas and Jean Pierre Pellissier, gathered in the Rollands' hut, while some slept in their wagons or on grain bags laid in rows. Samuel was elected president of the Conference of French Missionaries of the Paris Evangelical Missionary Society (PEMS), a position he held for 20 years.

Elizabeth records that missionaries saw their business as the elimination of what she called 'powers of darkness, ignorance and heathenism as seen in the practices of polygamy, circumcision, the purchase of wives and superstition'.

They carried on with mission work, immersed in the native communities. Their children ate what she called 'the coarse food of the natives', while the missionaries ate springbok, eland or gnu, some fish from the river and wild fowl Samuel had shot. Locusts became a constant challenge ruining harvests every year to perpetuate famine. Samuel relied on 'Providence' for survival.

He used a verse from the Lord's Prayer: 'Give us this day our daily bread' to inculcate a childlike trust, love and reverence in God. The inhabitants would mock the missionaries when they left church and pointed at their gardens destroyed by locusts and called Samuel 'false' because this misfortune was allowed by the God he praised.

Elizabeth writes that the inhabitants believed that the Great Spirit, which they called Modimo, was evil and the sole cause of all sickness, want, war and death. Some missionaries adopted the name of Jehovah to mitigate the local ideas concerning the Modimo (God) of the Bible. Calling Him Jehovah and not Modimo was to give Him a different identity and enable Africans to view Him in a different light – as a God of love and not of destruction.

* * *

The arrival of one Aaron Arends from Kuruman as an assistant to Samuel lifted the missionary's spirits: a multitalented handyman who could not only assist with building, but who was 'pleasant and affectionate' in demeanour.

Arends was a mason, carpenter, gardener and blacksmith. He built a cottage for his family and helped Basotho improve their beehive-like huts.

The number of people volunteering to be converted increased and an evening service at the chapel was crowded with souls wanting to be saved. Elizabeth wrote that so popular were these services that candles were brought to the chapel so that the service would not be cut short due to darkness. The sound of the French horn attracted even the shepherds who rushed down the hills for the services.

Word spread and more people flocked to Beersheba to witness the growing, thriving and flourishing settlement. And the school also grew, resulting in Arends building another class. Elizabeth acquired a native assistant teacher who was given the name Mary Jackson, apparently in 'remembrance of her great goodness'.

Converts, who became known as the 'first fruits' of the Rollands' work, became literate and fanatical in their overzealous uptake of

Christian values and practices. The conversions were remarkable. Samuel worked from daybreak into the night with the converts and new people seeking 'salvation'.

In her words, Elizabeth records that 'the lion became lamblike, the wolf turned into a pattern of gentleness, the blasphemer became a humble worshipper, and our wilderness truly began to rejoice'.

The missionary work was arduous and there were many challenges. Not all Basotho were welcoming, yet the Rollands managed to secure a settlement of over 2 000 inhabitants under Samuel's leadership. His persistence was remarkable. Perhaps converts began to see some value in being Christian – the ability to read and write, and to access the gospel of assurance must have resonated with them.

* * *

Elizabeth's reports attest to enormous activity at Beersheba. She superintended the operations of sowing seed, planting, watering and crop gathering. She gave attention to the care of the flocks, and to milking and shearing. The station sought to procure better houses – the beehive-like huts were replaced by hartebeest huts, which provided better heat retention in winter but stayed cool in summer – and they were furnished with tables and chairs. European clothing became common. The inhabitants used their fresh produce to acquire furniture from traders and the English shops in the Colony. An estimation by missionary Reverend Francois Daumas showed that from this station alone, the nearest town of Smithfield gained four thousand pounds in value or money in a year.

Some 50 ploughs were in constant use to cultivate the fields and richer converts owned about 30 wagons between them. The district was filled with fruit trees; wheat and corn were sown for at least about 30 kilometres in every direction. There were no reports of misconduct from the station as the inhabitants lived in comfort and prosperity. In spite of this, the Boers alleged that there was theft, though they were unable to provide any proof.

Historian David Coplan documented: 'Under missionary direction, Black Christian artisans trained others to build remarkable houses and public buildings, including a primary school, displaying fine stone craftsmanship constructed from local materials. The school accommodating 200 children was the first in the area. Books for the school were printed in Cape Town and then at Beersheba itself. In addition a church and a mission house were built; and here were tailoring and leatherworking facilities. Christian practical education proved to be an effective vehicle for both conversion and community-building.'

Pioneering for its time, the mission published a newspaper, *Moboleli oa Litaba* ('The Clarion'), in Sesotho in 1841 – a first for the territory – targeting the emerging Black Christian literate. It tackled religious matters and mission activity in the district. More than 800 people could read well and a few could speak Dutch and English with a small number conversant in French.

This was how success looked for the Rolland missionary undertaking.

15

The blood of Beersheba

Yet, for all its successes as a citadel of progress and excellence, Rolland's Beersheba would have a tragic and sudden end. One report called what happened at Beersheba 'one of the most awful and wicked actions that had ever taken place'.

* * *

Encircled by armed Boers ready to unleash their wrath, residents of the enclave were given a few minutes before a wholesale shooting spree ensued.

By the time the cannons and the guns ceased fire, gun powder hung thickly in the air and the mountains reverberated with the echoes of the roaring weapons.

Black bodies drenched in blood were strewn across the land.

Dismembered and torn limbs bore testimony of the merciless crack-of-dawn carnage that befell the unsuspecting community. The over 2 000 bodies would never be buried. Their graves were the stomachs of wild animals and birds of prey that feasted on them.

Counting the devastating losses beyond human life: over 5 000 cattle, 4 000 sheep, 500 horses and countless goats were stolen. Pigs and poultry were shot down. Crops were burned or were cut down and carried off.

Large sums of money were stolen. Male clothing was burned

and female garments carried off. Books were burned in a bonfire. Houses were pillaged and burned to the ground. The school building and the mission house survived.

The wagons of those who had fled in the night were overtaken the following day. Old men were killed, women were stripped and thrown into the river, their Bibles destroyed and wagons burned. The able-bodied men who had run away to the kloof were hunted down and killed.

The marauding Boers were repulsed when a group of armed young men of the station made a stand at the river. The Boers thought it was a force coming against them from Lesotho and they ran back to the destroyed mission station.

* * *

This bloodcurdling account of the murder of African Christians in 1858, which I read in an article by David Coplan, has haunted me.

The commandos were insatiable, merciless and brutal as they executed their murderous expedition before sunrise on Beersheba, a bustling citadel of Black excellence under the tutelage of French missionary Samuel Rolland. It was part of the first Basotho Boer War or Free State–Basotho War, which was over territorial rights. The Boers turned against Rolland. Their numbers had increased, and they could go against what Moshoeshoe had decided in terms of their stay in his land. They were also unhappy to see Africans doing so well under the guidance of Rolland.

Elizabeth Rolland writes that the Boers were 'maddened by envy and rushed upon the unoffending people and snatched their belongings'.

After the Beersheba massacre of African Christians and the destruction of the mission station, Rolland was arrested by the

Boers. He was guilty of nothing. He had no case to answer and so they let him go, perhaps because they were sympathetic to a fellow White man.

And in one swoop, Beersheba and all that it had achieved, was wiped off the face of the earth.

Anthropologists like David Coplan have dug out the ruins to bring this bloodbath to the centre of discussions on Black Christian history.

My uncle, Takatso, has devoted time to looking into the Beersheba Massacre and writing about it. He corroborated most of what Coplan has documented.

* * *

Sitting in Takatso's farm house in Devon, Mpumalanga, one winter night, my uncle told me what his research had yielded.

Beersheba became a centre of progress, excellence and education in the eastern Orange Free State. The town was bigger than the Smithfield of today. It was more important than Bloemfontein. All the meetings of Moshoeshoe and the British government were held in Beersheba, not in Bloemfontein, which was just a garrison for the British on guard for the Orange Free State sovereignty.

The seminary for Kereke ya Fora was in Beersheba. The missionaries trained teachers and ministers there.

In the early hours of 23 March 1858, Beersheba Mission Station was attacked by Boer burghers under the leadership of Johannes Sauer, the landdrost of Smithfield, acting on instructions from Jacobus Nicolaas Boshoff, the president of the Orange Free State republic.

The republic had voted to declare war on Basotho on the west and east of the Mohokare in the name of Boer expansion in the

Free State. Their intention was to take the land that fell under Moshoeshoe's rule.

Boshoff had formally declared war and had informed Moshoeshoe. In preparation, he had written to George Grey, governor of the Cape Colony, requesting him to allow the Boers in the Cape Colony to join in this murder. Grey refused. Boshoff also invited the Boers under Paul Kruger to join and they agreed. Further invitation was extended to Boers under Andries Pretorius who also joined in along with burghers from Bloemfontein.

The unsuspecting, innocent and defenceless Basotho Christians residing in the mission station could never have predicted – or probably even have prepared for – the bloodshed that would befall them.

The Boers left Smithfield at 4 am heading for the mission station. Once there, they completely surrounded it with the instruction to kill every Mosotho, old and young, man and woman, sick and healthy, able-bodied and living with disability.

They instructed all of Beersheba to disarm even though they knew that the people were not armed. No Black person was allowed by law to import arms and ammunition. Only White people were allowed to do so.

Part of the instruction was to burn all the houses of Basotho, all the mission station buildings and all the equipment and products, which included books, manuscripts and hymn books. The command was also to steal all the crops in the gardens and food stored in the granaries and to burn every crop in all the fields of the Beersheba farms. Only Rolland and his family, their house and properties were to be spared.

All writers who describe this mass murder in detail state that the pretext was to disarm Basotho and give them no time to hand in whatever weapons some might have had. However, the victims were not warned that war had been declared on all Basotho and would have had no context with which to understand the killing that was about to ensue.

The Basotho were given five minutes to hand in all arms before the random firing started. Rolland said that some who hid in ravines were found and killed. All Basotho were killed and a systematic burning of all buildings ensued. Chiefs Moeletsi and Mooi, and Rolland were taken to Smithfield as prisoners.

Takatso said according to Moshoeshoe's account, some old women and sick people were also taken prisoner and marched to Smithfield. Thereafter all Basotho in all the Beersheba farms were hunted down and killed indiscriminately. All their houses were reduced to ash and their animals were stolen and driven to Smithfield where they were shared among the Boers.

A river of blood flowed through the village of Beersheba. The dead were left where they were killed.

Takatso said Moshoeshoe wrote a letter to Boshoff about this killing of the African Christians. He noted that as a 'heathen' he had attacked Sekonyela but he never burned down the church of Sekonyela's people. Boshoff, on the other hand, as a Christian, had burned down a church of the Africans. He questioned what kind of Christianity they practised.

No graves exist at Beersheba for the decent burial of Beersheba Christians.

And there is no memorial for the slaughter that took place there.

16

The reckoning

As I scavenge for clues in the ruins of Beersheba, the stench of blood and the echoes of gun fire are beyond the realm of living memory. I stand here as a practising Christian with a conflicted identity.

I was brought up in the NG Kerk, a church that birthed and justified apartheid. My family – Black people, the very people it helped a cruel government oppress in too many ways to name – has devoted its life to this church for decades. I carry on this legacy of fidelity towards this church. It has morphed into the Uniting Reformed Church of Southern Africa (URCSA). It has denounced apartheid and called it a sin against humanity.

These conflicting, difficult truths trouble me.

Yet they live in me, in my blood.

My grandfather Mongangane was an evangelist of the NG Kerk. My uncle Takatso is a retired minister. My other uncle Jerry is a retired evangelist. My late father, Moses, served as an elder at the Pokello congregation in Katlehong. My two other uncles, Spanky and Bernard, were elders in Itsoseng, Lichtenburg when they were still alive.

* * *

We grew up calling the church Kereke ya Fora though. Literally translated, that means Church of France or French Church. Why

'French', when the church comes from the Netherlands, when it is known as the Dutch Reformed Church in English?

For years, no one could provide answers.

What we know for sure is that the Dutch Reformed Church is rooted in the politics of Afrikanerdom. From the days of Helpmekaar and Broederbond in the wake of the Boer War (1899 to 1902) and the World War I (1914 to 1918), Afrikaners needed to assert their identity and authority, and the church was at the heart of its project.

The separation of races was implemented in the early days of the church, and it never ceased to justify this racism. In spite of this, its membership grew among Black members.

The NG Kerk in South Africa had what became known as 'daughter churches' that were demarcated along racial lines. The mother church was for Whites, NG Kerk in Afrika for Blacks, NG Kerk Sending for the Coloureds, and NG Kerk Mission for the Indians.

By implication, the non-White races in the NG Kerk were in bed with the perpetrators of apartheid, their oppressors. One cannot help but think of Stockholm syndrome, which is defined in the *Penguin Dictionary of Psychology* as 'an emotional bond between hostages and their captors', a phenomenon often observed when hostages are held for a long time under emotionally straining circumstances.

In their communities, the members of the NG Kerk were seen as sell-outs because they attended the apartheid church. On the ambiguity of being Black and reformed, Allan Boesak wrote: 'The God of the Reformed Tradition was the God of slavery, fear, persecution and death. Yet for those Black Christians this was the God to whom they had to turn to for comfort, for justice, for peace.'

Many years later, and after a few facelifts, the NG Kerk in Afrika

The reckoning 145

has a new name, Uniting Reformed Church in Southern Africa, but what has changed?

* * *

In Alexandra township in Johannesburg, I sit in the front pews where the men's ministry of the church sits. It's the same church that was once led by struggle stalwart Reverend Sam Buti of the Save Alexandra Campaign. It is the same church that provided a refuge to Reverend Beyers Naudé when he was ostracised for his unpopular views against Afrikaner domination. Interestingly, William Nicol, after whom a busy road in Johannesburg is named, was once a minister in this very church in the 1960s.

We still recite the Apostles' Creed; we worship and sing hymns that glorify the grace of God, just as we did in the NG Kerk of old. The White ministers may be in short supply, but the legacy of a church steeped in Afrikaans remains. There are Black ministers of the church elsewhere who are known to still deliver sermons wholly in Afrikaans or peppered with Afrikaans to their entirely African congregations.

Even in church communication, the church continues to opt for Afrikaans over English. A ward, commonly known as home cell in today's churches, is known as a *wyk* in ours; the place where the minister and the church council meet before a service is known as the *konsistorie*; the holy communion is known as *nagmaal*; the church council is called the *kerkraad*. The Afrikaans imprint is everywhere, as ever, in the Reformed religion as practised by African Christians.

Perhaps to them, Afrikaans was a lingua franca of their predecessors and doesn't carry the burden and shame of being associated with racial supremacy. Could it be that these Christians take on a different cloak when they enter the grounds of the church, and when they return to their communities, they become vociferous opponents of the language? Sometimes, religion forces us to take a different view of matters from how we may be socialised.

How did we get here?

The author, second from right, is a member of the men's ministry of the church. He is seen here singing from the *Hosanna* hymnbook of the NG Kerk, now used in the URCSA, at his home congregation of Alexandra, Johannesburg. Photo: Family Album

As I retrace the steps of Mongangane, a cardinal figure in my life and the one who changed the trajectory of my family's destiny, I have walked down meandering corridors of history picking up clues, connecting dots and making inferences. He was missionary educated, the first to be literate and numerate in the entire family tree, and he went on to have a successful career as an evangelist and missionary.

He set us, his descendants, on the path to success and we are able to pluck the fruits of education that came with having an educated patriarch who was also an influential community leader. Many doors may not have opened for us had we not been the sons and daughters of the evangelist on a scooter. We got to sit in the front rows of churches and high tables with the rich and royal in recognition of our grandfather's status.

Be that as it may, I have this niggling issue of the highly problematic church he gave his service to, and that leaves me conflicted.

I asked Takatso to explain and account for how he and his brothers came to serve in the NG Kerk, something I see as an oxymoron, a contradiction in terms. I mean, he, Takatso, is an exponent of Black Theology rooted in the Black Consciousness and Black Power of the 1970s, yet he served in a church that overtly supported the oppression of Black people.

It was at the height of Black Theology of the 1970s that voices within the NG Kerk in Afrika and in the Sendingskerk began to grow louder and braver in opposition to the mother church's stance of continued justification of apartheid, Takatso reminds me. The daughter churches declared apartheid a sin and, by association, their mother had sinned in her stance on this shameful human rights violation.

In 1994, the offspring of the NG Kerk cut ties with the mother and struck out as the URCSA. They introduced the Belhar Confession, which took a stand against segregation and other human rights violations.

The move to URCSA was not peaceful. Some congregations, mostly in the Free State and North West provinces of South Africa resisted the change, leading to sporadic clashes that became physical and police intervention was sought. There were court cases over property and recognition of the NG Kerk. The relationship was somehow mended in 2015 through a settlement and the arbitration of the mother church. Talks are ongoing to unite the URCSA and the remaining NG Kerk congregations.

Takatso's answers pointed me to another alley of history and answered the other question I had about the church's French connection.

In 1833, the young French missionaries Eugene Casalis, Thomas Arbousset and Constand Gosselin arrived at Thaba Bosiu to meet King Moshoeshoe I. This meeting began a new chapter for Basotho. Christianity was put at the centre of their existence. Literacy was introduced, but so were Western values, mores and practices, which were often at loggerheads with African culture. This set the nation on a collision course as it confronted the evolution of the new social pact.

We have to understand how Christianity was introduced to African communities or, more specifically, how the idea of a church became a cornerstone of the African lived experience.

We go to church religiously, sing hymns, worship and share the Word with fervour and excitement, despite its fundamental clash with our ancestral histories, but how did we get here?

17
The church

The church has become a central feature in our lives. It occupies an imposing presence in our Sunday (or Saturday) schedule. For some of us who were brought up in the church, to skip a service is to invite feelings of guilt. The church – and the duties and responsibilities that surround it – has been ingrained in our psyche to the extent that we have come to accept it as a natural.

How did that happen? How did religion reach our shores and how did the concept of a church become such a necessary and unquestioned aspect of our existence?

Many of us turn to the church for the communal experience. We do accept that church attendance in and by itself doesn't guarantee that one will see heaven. It takes a lot more of your faith and spiritual practice to even be considered worthy to be the child of God. But still, church plays an important role in the physical realm. Worshipping together with other believers, belting out hymns and holding hands together in communion, brings a reassurance of togetherness and brotherhood or sisterhood. We are united in faith. We are family beyond family.

However, Christianity has been around us for about 2 000 years, so it's a relatively new phenomenon for Africans. By the turn of the 19th century, Islam was the dominant form of monotheism in Africa. Christianity existed in small enclaves on the coast in the Congo basin and on the Zambezi.

The African church history remains overlooked and understudied.

There are loads of books on Christianity and the work of missionaries in Africa, yet Black church history, which has its own narrative and nuances, and which would be best captured by the people who practise Christianity, has largely not been documented.

Professors JF Ade Ajayo and EA Ayandele argued that church history has been written as if the Christian church were in Africa, but not of Africa. Church history has stressed the missionary presence, forgetting or neglecting whatever there was of an African initiative.

* * *

The first missionary enterprise dates back to 1799 when JT van der Kemp, a medical doctor from Holland with a degree from Edinburgh arrived as an agent of the London Missionary Society. Before this, the White settlers had their church services but without the missionary component. His earliest converts included the Griqua and the Mfengu who fled their homes during Difaqane.

Another missionary was a Scot called John Phillip. His efforts were not immediately successful and conversion numbers remained low. Christians were in the minority in places such as the Zululand areas where kings tolerated missionaries for diplomatic and other reasons.

Robert Moffat, a 22-year-old Scottish Congregationalist, found a welcoming people when he settled in Kuruman and established a thriving mission among Batswana. He even wrote down the language and was the first person to translate the Bible into Setswana by the 1850s. He'd come to Africa as part of a youth movement. These missionaries were young and footloose and took to the new Christian message. Some of them were sent to West Africa and, due to the climate, died within days, months or a few years. Others found the climate of South Africa and parts of East Africa hospitable and stayed on for half a century or more in some cases.

King Moshoeshoe of Basotho invited the Paris Evangelical Missionary Society, which was first represented by Eugene Casalis, Thomas Arbousset and Constand Gosselin, in 1833. They met in Thaba Bosiu and held services there before moving southwards to Morija, which became a bigger station. The presence of the missionaries was for economic and diplomatic reasons, in addition to the work they did in education and literacy.

The initial contact between the people in southern Africa and European missionaries was, in a way, a controlled negotiated strategic relationship in which Africans acted in good faith, as people had done for centuries, trading and exchanging goods and knowledge. To begin with, the power was far more in the hands of the hosts than the incomers, who were graciously allowing contact, but with conditions of trade and exchange. It was through violent greed that the power tipped over. And it was thanks to the hospitality of Africans that missionary work succeeded. There were other communities that were less welcoming and where missions failed.

As historian, author and champion of the New African Movement Ntongela Masilela explains, it was truly extraordinary the way the missionaries learned the linguistic structure of many languages so that they could translate the Bible into a multiplicity of African tongues. In so doing, not only did they enhance literacy and the reading of literary texts, but they also began constructing the understanding of the linguistic structure of African languages. It must be noted, however, that they sought largely to confine the historical and intellectual imagination of the emergent New Africans solely around the horizon of the Bible.

Casalis became a trusted aide of Moshoeshoe and wrote some

of the letters King Moshoeshoe sent to authorities in the other colonies negotiating for his territory and other rights. The missionaries became central to the national and educational experience of Basotho.

Among the Batswana, rulers like Khama, who led Bamangwato from 1875 to 1923, and Sechele, became Christians under the influence of the Berlin and Hermannsburg Lutherans who were active in the Cape, Transvaal and Botswana. But by the 20th century many Batswana remained traditionalists. Many more Africans resisted and held on to their traditional practices than converted. In some cases, they juggled the traditions that contradicted Christian teachings (such as initiation, bride price and consulting traditional healers and sangomas) with their new Western religion. Some Africans were simply indifferent to the gospel.

While the mission enterprise brought some success, the numbers were small.

In 1911, over 30 missionary societies and 1 650 missionaries were in operation in South Africa, making the country the most occupied mission field on the continent. Yet, decades later only a relatively small of number of converts could be counted. Robert Moffat was quoted as saying that he had fewer Christians than fruit trees.

David Livingstone, who had come to South African in 1841 as a missionary for the London Mission Society, was based in Botswana among the BaKgatla, but left the station in 1845, discouraged by the poor conversion rate in his southern Tswana mission station. Livingstone rose to prominence with his subsequent exploration into southern and central Africa. He named the Mosi-oa-Thunya waterfalls Victoria Falls after the British Queen Victoria, and he pushed the colonialism and imperialism agenda in his travels.

Converts to Christianity of any flavour did not have an easy ride.

On the one hand, the converts were often ostracised and faced persecution by the people they had come from. On the other, they were discriminated against by their White fellow believers. An African Methodist quoted in 1863 said, 'To the natives we are but despised believers, to the English we are no more than kaffirs.'

It wasn't until African evangelists were employed that the expansion of Christianity took hold in the 20th century. It would seem that Africans were persuaded better by the missionaries that looked like them and who spoke their language. And yet, when it comes to stories of missionary work, one always hears the same names of that first generation of missionaries from the 19th century – people like Moffat, Casalis and Livingstone.

It is reported that as foreigners, the missionaries found their way into communities through the chiefs. Some of the chiefs mistrusted the White people and they refused to be baptised. King Moshoeshoe, for instance, had a decades-long history of working with the missionaries, was a regular churchgoer, and a practising Christian, yet he died unbaptised. Among the first generation of rulers to be baptised was Chief Kama of the Gqunukwebe Xhosa.

The chiefs saw the presence of missionaries in African communities as beneficial for them to have contact with the European government. In the case of Batswana, as early as 1823 they experienced 'rescue' from a missionary. Details of what happened to which community are unclear, but it is believed there was a rumour that a community that accepted a missionary into its midst could not be defeated in war. It was believed that this powerful White man had cosmological influence with the Almighty, Giver or Withholder of Rain.

It helped that missionaries brought with them tools that made life easier, like ploughs, and Western medicines. These added to their influence and power over Africans.

Mission stations introduced new landmarks on the African landscape. Chapels, the catechism class, school, the printing press and the lodges for children who lived far started to assert church discipline, regimentation and the enforcement of rules, and these began to be absorbed, submissively or reluctantly.

Change was on the horizon everywhere. The White Cape settler community of Dutch origin was self-contained and comfortable in its isolation in the 1790s. When the Dutch East India Company rule ended and the British took control, the fate of the Cape and southern Africa was determined by the British. The European settler population moved from around Cape Town into the interior and introduced stock-raising, wheat-growing and viticulture. They needed more land to expand their enterprises, and this resulted in constant territorial expansion putting them at loggerheads with African communities already settled in the surrounding areas. Violence was inevitable.

Before the English takeover, the Dutch Reformed Church – the NG Kerk – was the state church. Preachers were appointed by the Dutch Company in Amsterdam. There were seven congregations in Cape Town and Graaff-Reinet by 1795. Mission work in the Dutch Reformed Church among the Boers took root as early as the 1780s with the work of Helperus van Lier and Michiel Vos who challenged the consciences of some Whites to consider the need for evangelising the Khoi.

The powerful *kerkraad* (church council), made up of elders and deacons headed by influential Boers in the community, set the rules of engagement. Other races were accommodated in the Dutch Reformed Church initially, but the scales of power tilted towards the Boers from the very start.

Coloured servants, for instance, sat on the floor as they took part in the daily evening worship with the Boer family. The patriarchal head of the household would read a sermon, followed by a prayer, from Conrad Mel or Johannes Haverman's prayer books. On Sunday mornings the same audience would be treated to a bigger sermon.

The *nagmaal* (holy communion) was held quarterly. It still is. Agreement was reached at the 1829 synod that the *nagmaal* would be shared by all Christians regardless of colour. In practice, however, that was not the case and congregations ignored the rule.

Almost thirty years later, at the 1857 synod, the tune had changed completely when separation was officially instituted. The church, using the pious phrase 'for the sake of Christ's cause and owing to the weakness of some', enforced separate worship. The result was the establishment of the Dutch Reformed Mission Church in 1881, which was for Coloureds only.

Andrew Murray, the South African-born son of a Dutch Reformed missionary from Scotland, was a trained theologian who had become more interested in the charismatic approach he discovered when he went to Europe and experienced the evangelical revival. He founded a missionary institute for lay preachers in Wellington and published many books on spirituality. He became an internationally revered religious figure.

Murray's work, views and message revived the Dutch Reformed Church around 1860 and inspired it to embark on a full-scale missionary activity.

The church looked to Europe for missionaries and seemed to see no place for Africans in its mission plans. They might have groomed local missionaries, but they did not. What this did was to link the church roots and ties with Europe and pitch the religion as foreign to Africans.

In the Cape, after the British takeover, some Dutch Reformed military and colonial chaplains went over to the new state church and signed up on short-term appointments in it. Their congregation consisted of civil servants and soldiers. Anglican bishops and priests paid brief visits on their way to India or Australia. They would minister to their English brothers and sisters. The Anglican Church was not present in South Africa until the first Bishop of Cape Town, Robert Gray, arrived in 1848.

The Roman Catholic Church had its first bishop stationed in the Cape in 1838.

In other words, for the first four decades of the 19th century, the Dutch Reformed Church monopolised Christianity at the Cape and its surrounding settlements. The story would be vastly different a century later with the Catholic and Anglo-Catholic communities dominating.

One analysis of church history points to the fact that earlier interpretations of church beginnings in the Cape do not bring to light the considerable difference between the work among the Coloureds in the south west of the Cape and that among the Bantu-speaking Africans further east.

It is argued that it is important to remember that the Coloured Christian groups, especially the Griquas, were intermediary agents in the evangelisation of Bantu-speaking communities. The Khoi-Coloured communities were increasingly alienated from White society at the Cape. However they were to play an essential role as a bridge for the evangelisation of some of the Bantu-speaking peoples.

The Boers increased their pace as they moved deeper into the interior and established the Transvaal and Orange Free State republics. The Voortrekkers, Calvinistic and conservative, who did a lot of this frontier work, insisted that there would be no equality in the church and state between White and Black. This ideal would permeate rural South Africa in the 19th century and the urban environment of the 20th century and have a lasting impact in the Dutch Reformed Church for generations.

Ernest Cole in his iconic *House of Bondage* book, which was written at the height of apartheid and was subsequently banned, calls the mission of Christianity to South Africa a schizoid experience. He argued that there was no place on earth where Christianity was so at odds with itself and pursued in contrasting words. 'It was in the name of Christianity that apartheid was rationalised and defended, yet it was in its name that apartheid was condemned,' he wrote.

He explained that European and American missionaries preached separation in the church and that Whites would hold all positions of responsibility in churches and it was only in Black churches that African Christians could express themselves. He quoted the NG Kerk as the most extreme with its teaching of apartheid as an integral part of Christianity. 'The early Boer settlers brought with them a Calvinist belief in predestination – that salvation cannot be earned by good works but is limited to the "elect" of God. They were the elect and they thought of God not as a Spirit of Unity, but as the Great Divider.'

This superiority complex has cost South Africa so much. Instead of seeking integration and tolerance, Christianity was weaponised. It brought so much strife in the day-to-day African experience.

18

The French connection and the Boer influence

The mellifluous voices that fill the church convey a sense of community in a magical way. It is a marvel to watch and hear unrehearsed voices create a harmony that lifts up your spirits and transports you to a place where peace and harmony reign and pain is defeated. Isn't that the land of promise where honey and milk flow?

The words jump out of the *Hosanna* hymnbook and waft in the air inviting a passer-by and comforting the downtrodden in the pews.

But what are we singing? Where do these songs come from? What do they have to do with the French Church and the French missionaries that brought Christianity to Basotho. I believe that revisiting these hymns will provide clues and dots we can connect and make a link about the origins of the church.

The singing of hymns is central to most gatherings, feasts, funerals and celebrations. These hymns found their own way into African culture without us necessarily understanding their origins. They have been handed over to children by parents for generations without much context or knowledge about where they come from, who composed them or even understanding of their lyrics.

* * *

Hosanna is the hymnbook used in the Black NG Kerk and serves as a practical artefact and remnant that gives clues about the French connection.

Even with a new name, the Uniting Reformed Church has kept the liturgy of the NG Kerk in Afrika as well as the *Hosanna*. In the foreword of the *Hosanna*, dated 1966, HCS van der Merwe, the chairman of the hymnbook commission, noted that for years the church used the hymnbooks of other churches, such as *Lifela tsa Sione tsa Tirelo ea Molimo mo Kereken le Sekolen*, published by the Religious Tract Society in 1907 in Setswana. Boasting 361 hymns, it became known as *Kopelo* in 1920.

The isiZulu hymnbook used in the isiZulu-speaking congregation, known as *Dumisani*, was arranged by Reverend LHM Jandrell, whereas the isiXhosa version *Incwadi Yamaculo* used in the isiXhosa-speaking congregation was arranged by Reverend JC Oosthuysen.

The General Synod of the NG Kerk in Afrika set up a commission to curate a new hymnbook in different languages on 17 August 1953. This resolution was passed on to the non-White church synod in May 1959 and the four synods chose their respective commissions, which started work in October of the same year.

The general synod of the non-White churches resolved that the Sesotho version would be the responsibility of the Orange Free State synod, and in 1959 a ten-member commission was set up, chaired by BW Zietsman with HCS van der Merwe as the secretary. Zietsman noted that the translation of the hymns proved to be an arduous and painstaking task that took them four years.

The *Hosanna* was adopted on 30 March 1966 in Bloemfontein. It was translated in Sesotho, Sepedi, Setswana, isiZulu and isiXhosa. It included 111 hymns taken from *Lifela tsa Sione* from the Morija Sesutu Book Depot and they are clearly marked as such in the *Hosanna*. Some of the hymns were translated from the mother church hymnbook.

The *Hosanna* also included classical compositions: Joseph

Haydn's *The Heavens Are Telling*, translated to Sesotho as *Kganya Ya Modimo*; and George Frideric Handel's *Halleluya Chorus* translated as *Lehlaso la Dihalleluya*, and his *Holy is the Lord* translated as *O a Halalela Morena*.

But to the families that accepted Christianity for generations, the hymns of *Lifela tsa Sione* carry a spiritual bond that cannot be broken. Their ancestors are the original singers of *lifela* (hymns) dating back to the 1830s and 40s. It was at the feet of their great-grandparents that these hymns, that were passed down from generation to generation, were learned. On Sunday afternoons after the service, my grandmother would sit me down to practise *lifela*.

* * *

The origins of the generic name *sefela* (plural: *lifela* or *difela*) – equivalent of a Christian hymn – are traced back to the work of the London missionary Robert Moffat who worked among Batlhaping in present-day Kuruman and Taung, and in Basutoland. Moffat appropriated the term *sehela* (a variant spelling of *sefela*) from the Batlhaping, who used it for the sacred initiation songs similar to those known as *likoma* by Basotho.

Coplan put it this way: ever seeking to steal the heathen's thunder, Moffat took the term with him when he went to work in Basutoland in 1830, where the word was given the local form *sefela*. The linking quality between *likoma* and *lifela* was a 'moral emotionality' – the songs were 'cries of the heart', as some Basotho commentators have said.

Lifela tsa Sione means 'Hymns of Zion', and it was first published in 1854. The hymns the book contains were originally composed by the French missionaries in Lesotho: Eugene Casalis, Constand Gosselin, Francois Coillard, Thomas Arbousset, Adolphe Mabille, and

Samuel and Elizabeth Rolland who were from the Reformed church. When these missionaries got to Lesotho, ancestral worship was robust. The teaching from the songs found a home in the hymns they composed.

They also adapted hymns from *Chants de Sion* by César Malan, a renowned Christian hymn writer with over 1 000 hymns to his name who was born in Geneva in 1787.

Malan, as the originator of the modern hymn movement in the French Reformed Church, composed hymns perpetuated in the analysis of the Christian experience. The hymns were set to his own melodies. He was an artist and a mechanic; his little workshop had its own printing press.

By the time the French missionary work ended in the 1920s or so, a good number of Basotho were literate and numerate, and had attained appreciable levels of Western civilisation and 'sophistication'. Thekiso Khati, a scholar at the National University of Lesotho, argued that this was achieved through the educational, religious, political and diplomatic efforts of the missionaries. He offered that Lesotho was indebted to the missionaries for laying the foundation of the country's formal Western education.

* * *

The compositions of *Lifela tsa Sione*, which have been adopted by other Protestant denominations in Lesotho and beyond, were influenced by the late-19th-century Victorian myth of the Dark Continent, that shaped the thinking of colonisers and missionaries alike.

In his critical article, 'Postcolonial Reading of Nineteenth-Century Missionaries' Musical Texts: The Case of *Lifela tsa Sione* and *Lifela tsa Bakriste*, Paul Leshota of the University of Lesotho posited that underlying this myth was the predominant thought that Africa was an embodiment of savagery, intractable ignorance, and callous barbarity, and that it was the epicentre of evil. The assumed cultural superiority that underpinned the missionary attitude was not a far-fetched idea. 'It was the very air that people at the time breathed.'

Prior to their coming to Africa, the missionaries were prepared and strengthened for the task that awaited them. Rigorous training consisted of Latin, Greek, classical literature, philosophy, as well as theological training. Of course, the training made no accommodation or space for local cultures. It did not allow for coexistence, cross-pollination or tolerance of how Africans had lived for centuries. It was all about the European agenda that eventually culminated in full-scale imperialism and colonisation.

As soon as they arrived, missionaries wasted no time in rooting out what they perceived as 'paganism' among the Basotho, which was, in their view, a great obstacle to the progress of the gospel of Christ. There was a clear divide between what the 'pagans' and what the missionaries understood as pagan customs and practices. Missionaries were, for example, vehemently opposed the cultural practices of bohadi, polygamy and initiation, and new converts were expected to shun their centuries-old way of life in exchange for the White man's view of the world, which was presented as superior and morally upright. Some who resisted conversion held it as non-negotiable to abandon their cultural practices and to don a 'White mask', to borrow a Frantz Fanon expression.

The destruction of non-Christian societies was a precondition for conversion. It was felt that, first you destroy the culture, then you can convert.

Leshota reminds us that missionaries called Basotho 'uncivilized people' and 'savages' in the letters they exchanged between themselves. This attitude, he argues, manifested in the hymns they composed for their African 'clients'. Over 180 years later, and in a new theological and political context, we continue to sing them with gullibility. Leshota warns that, not only were these texts at the service of the process of Christian conquest, but that they have also colluded with other imperialising texts to colonise, authorise and legitimise the subjugation of Basotho. Through these hymns, as imperialistic and imperialising texts, the Basotho are constructed in ways that fit and serve the imperialistic interests.

Over and above the so-called pagan traditional customs of initiation, polygamy and marriage by cattle – which missionaries spared no effort in rooting out – were issues linked to civilisation, which had a bearing on Christian decency and moderation. Among these issues were dance and music. However, because of their perceived associations with war, violence, ancestral feasts and other traditional rituals, music and dance were viewed with great suspicion by the missionaries.

When the missionaries introduced the hymns and taught them to the so-called heathens, it was part of a bigger project – that of rooting out pagan and 'savage' customs and replacing them with Christianity and civilisation. In the missionaries' purview, the Basotho music and songs served to promote and entrench the very customs that they wanted to root out.

It did not, therefore, come as a surprise that the missionaries, in more than one instance, expressed their joy that 'the wild dances and warlike songs' were no longer sung, and that 'savage songs have been succeeded by the Songs of Sion, and pagan customs by the Christian service'.

Leshota said these ideological texts reflect uneven power relations between the missioner and the missionarised: 'the so-called generous, lovable, courageous European crusades and martyrs on one side and the supposedly thinly veneered, heathen, barbarous African on the other.'

When the missionaries composed the hymns, they turned to Malan's *Chants de Sion* as a source of text and inspiration from which they translated into Sesotho. This, Leshota argues, turned Basotho into a poor imitation of Frenchmen in Africa.

They did, however, compose a new anthology rooted in hope and a promise of the afterlife, but in the process also exposed the biases of the missionaries.

The tunes and melodies were from Europe and served as the basis for the hymns across the denominational divide in Lesotho.

Leshota presented the first three stanzas of the Eugene Casalis composition, 'Jehova Molimo oa Iseraele', number 7 in *Lifela tsa Sione* along with their loose translations. This happens to be a popular hymn in the mutated Uniting Reformed Church where I'm a member.

1. Jehova Molimo oa Iseraele
U re falalitse lefifing la pele
Re thaba hakaakang ha re u khumamela
Kajeno re batho, re tseba ho rapela

2. Maoto a khotso a tsoang ho Monghali
A tlile Lesotho, lefatseng la mali
A re a sa hlaha, Satan'a thothomela
Mokhosi oa khutsa, lira tsa re bakela

3. Mahaheng a matso, thakong tsa lelimo
Ho binoa sefela se bokang Molimo
Naha ea nyakalla, e khabile ka metse
Nala e hlahile bakeng sa litsietsi

1. Yahweh, the God of Israel
You have snatched us from the ancient darkness
We are happy that we are able to worship you
Today we are human beings, we know how to pray

2. The peace-bearing feet from the Lord
Have come to Lesotho, the land of blood
As they approached, the devil trembles
The cry dies down, the enemies surrender/convert

3. In the dark caves, where the cannibals used to dwell
Hymns praising God are sung
The entire country, adorned with villages rejoices
There is abundance in place of misery

Leshota noted that the song had some historical nuance to it and reflected the missionary interpretation of the events that engulfed Lesotho at the time, such as the phenomenon of cannibalism. For some, barbaric as it may appear, it was an act by humans who were fighting for the survival of the human race, which was facing total extinction as a result of wars and famine. For others it was an unprecedented and unequalled act of barbarism.

The hymn displays dominant superstitions held by the Western world about Africa being a continent teeming with wild men and imaginary beasts.

The caves that are mentioned had become a common habitation for the cannibals who were spread in small bands throughout the country, from the south to the north, especially on the main route, waiting for their unsuspecting human prey.

The idea of cannibalism, even though it was not unknown in Europe, was often a scare tactic used in imperialism, and was a way of keeping the coloniser and the colonised apart, says Leshota. It was used as a form of othering of the darker-skinned inhabitants of colonised countries, regardless of whether or under which circumstances cannibalism actually took place.

Victorian novels and poetry of the 19th century exploited the fear of human-flesh-eating and other cruel misrepresentations of people who were not from Europe. Africa became a stage on which Europe could project its assumed superiority. Europe was light, was right, was good, says Leshota. Africa was dark, was wrong, was bad. People like the explorer David Livingstone and his antecedents, and the ones who followed him were seen as bearers of enlightenment, culture and sophistication to places where these were lacking, presuming only the worst about anyone who did not look, think, act or live as they did.

* * *

Here is another example of a hymn that makes problematic assumptions as highlighted by theology scholars Rantoa Letsosa and BJ de Klerk. It is hymn number 68 in *Lifela tsa Sione* and is called 'Lichaba Tsohle Tsa Lefatshe'. It was composed by Thomas Arbousset*.

Lichaba tsohle tsa lefatshe	All the nations of the world
Li tla tla Sioneng	Will come to Zion
Ba lutseng bochabela-tsatsi	Those in the east
Le bophirimeleng	And the west
Batho bohle ba tla phuthana	All the people will gather
Ho boka Morena	To praise the Lord
Ba tla lula, ba tla ratana	They will live and love each other
Ba lese ho loana	And stop fighting

*author's translation

The hymn is sung against the background of viewing Basotho as the lost tribe of Judah that somehow relates to the Arabs. The Basotho must come back to Zion, stop fighting and start living a peaceful and harmonious life. This song also testifies that the French missionaries had the belief that all are children of Abraham and also believed that there will once again be a reunion in the new Jerusalem and there will no longer be war.

* * *

Here is another hymn: 'Jo Lefifi Le Lekaakang' by Francois Coillard.

Jo lefifi le lekaakang	Oh what darkness
Le aparetseng lefatshe	Covering the world
Jo botsho bo hlomidisang	The frightening darkness
Le tla chaba neng letsatsi	When will the sun rise

Oho tsatsi la ho loka	Oh the good sun
Ke nako thuntsa mafube	It's time to dawn
Chaba fatsheng la Afrika	Over the land of Africa
Fatshe la madimabe	A land of misfortune

Hasa hasa phatlalatsa	Spread across
Sedi la hao le molemo	Your light of kindness
Phatsima benya phahama	Rise and shine
Tsatsi le letle la Ntate	The good sun of our father

It was possibly the darkness that enveloped Africa in the 1830s and 40s way before electricity was spoken of, that inspired the writing of this hymn, in which the composer identifies Africa as the dark continent of misfortune and bad luck where nothing good emerges until the sun rises. The sun is the arrival of the missionaries, and the gospel is presented as a doomed continent's saving grace. The composer calls Africa a land of misfortune, bad luck and backwardness. It is only when people accept Christianity that their fortunes may change. Holding on to their 'savage' beliefs and practices will only condemn them to darkness and doom. Again, the idea of whiteness and light is associated with Western religion and scorns everything that is Black, African and indigenous.

* * *

Hymn 89 by Samuel Rolland:

Se teng seliba sa mali	There is a well of blood
Aletereng ya tefelo	At the altar of sacrifice
Liba se eleng sehlare	The well of healing
Matl'a sona ke bophelo	Its strength is life
Baetsalibe ba batsho	The heathens in their darkness
Ba se kenang ka tumelo	They enter it with faith
Ba tloha teng ka bosoeu	And leave white
Ka thabo le ka tshoarelo	With joy and forgiveness

This is one of the most popular hymns sung in celebration of conversion and salvation. The second stanza associates heathens with darkness. One may even offer that it could be one of those instances where everything black and dark was associated with the devil, whereas whiteness is associated with purity and goodness. In fact the third line of the second stanza is telling: it says that after salvation, these black heathens emerge 'white', joyful and forgiven of their sins. It is a loaded statement that invokes feelings of disdain and dislike for blackness and extols virtues of whiteness.

* * *

Other popular hymns engender the spirit of hope and a promise of the afterlife. Hymns such as 'Ke Na Le Molisa', 'Ha Le Mpotsa Tshepo Yaka' and 'Re Ya Ho Boka Morena' are sung by some of the biggest names in gospel like Lebo Sekgobela, Winnie Mashaba, Joyous Celebration, Tshepo Tshola, IPCC, ZCC Mokhukhu, Amadodana ase Wesile, Soweto Gospel Choir, Sechaba and Barorisi ba Morena.

Gospel music is a big industry by any measure and accounts for 40 per cent of music sold in South Africa. Central to the genre are the hymns. In paying close attention to the words of these hymns, one is aware of their poetic beauty, but also of the missionaries' unshakeable faith in God.

* * *

Hymn 111 by Samuel Rolland:

Ke na le molisa	The Lord is my shepherd
Ke tla be ke hlokang	I shall not want
Ke ea ipitsang Jehova	He calls himself Jehova
Molimo o phelang	The living God
O nkisa botaleng	He leads me to green pastures
Lijong tse mphelisang	Where I get nourishing food
O nkalosa linokaneng	He leads me by still waters
Metsing a nkholisang	By sweet waters

Ha ke lahlehile	When I am lost
O nkhutlisetsa hae	He leads me back home
O nkisa tseleng ya 'nete	He leads me to the way of truth
Ka lerato la hae	With his love
Ha ke se ke feta	As I pass
Kgohlong e lefifi	In the dark valley
Ha nka ke ka tsoha tsela	I'm not worried by the road
E chehiloeng lifi	Full of traps
Lira li ka ntlhoea	My enemies may detest me
Ke sa ja monono	I am fulfilled
Mohope oa khaphatsheha	My cup runs over
Ke dutse ka thabo	I am joyous
U sa tla mpaballa	He will keep me safe
Le bophelong bona	In this life
'Me ke tla hlola ka mehla	And I will spend the rest of my days
Ka tlung ea Morena	In the house of the Lord

'Ke Na Le Molisa' is inspired by the Psalm 23, which begins with the words 'The Lord is my Shepherd'. Rolland shows dexterity around the Sotho language. He wove a hymn that has become a staple, and which might actually be the most popular hymn from *Lifela tsa Sione* sung across denominations.

* * *

Hymn 108 by Eugene Casalis:

Ha le mpotsa tsepo ea ka	When you ask me who shall I trust
Ke tla re ke Jesu	I will say it is Jesus
Ke lapetse ho mo aka	I long to embrace him
Ha hae ke ha eso	His home is my home
Ka na ka nyoreloa botle	I thirst for goodness
Ka tsoatsoa ke batla	I went to look
Ka tsieloa ke ntho tsohle	I was troubled by everything
Ka felloa ke matla	I lost all my strength
Athe Jesu o n'a mpona	Jesus saw me
Ha ke lela joalo	As I was crying
A mpitsa a re: Tlo ho'na	He called out to me: Come to me
U fole matsoalo	And be at ease
Joale ke kgotse ka mehla	Now I am filled
Mohau wa Modimo	By the grace of God
Ke qadile ho iketla	I started to be content
Tsepong ea holimo	With the hope of heavens

This hymn is about hope and trust in the Lord. It is only in Him that I will find comfort and peace. I long to be with him, I wish to be one with him. In my moment of vulnerability, want and lack He saw me and gave me comfort. Since knowing God and being under His grace I have known peace.

* * *

Hymn 12 by Samuel Rolland:

Rea u boka Morena	We praise you Lord
Re ntse re thabela uena	We are happy in your presence
Re sa phela ha monate	We are still good
Ka paballo ea hao, Ntate	Under your protection, oh Father
Re pholositsoe ka mohau	We were saved by grace
Ka lineo tsohle tsa hao	With gifts from you
Reko la hao le leholo	Your grace is generous
Le re thabisitse pelo	It has pleased our hearts
Khanna joale bana ba hao	Now lead your children
Ba ee ka taba tsa molao	To go by your ways
E be joko e bobebe	May it be a light burden
E sikoarang ka sebete	They carry bravely
U re nee ho thabela	Let us be happy
Tsee u li ratang kaofela	To accept all that you want
Thato ea hao e phethehe	May your will be done
Bana ba hao ba khethehe	Your children be special

This is a devotion to the peace and protection believers enjoy in the presence of God. It declares that we are born-again converts who enjoy the privileges of His grace. It gives an undertaking to commit to God's will in exchange for being in His flock as His special child, the chosen ones.

* * *

Hymn 53 by Eugene Casalis:

Joko ea hao e bobebe	Your yoke is light
E nkhatholola pelo	It puts my heart at ease
Tumelo ho 'na ke thebe	My faith is a shield
E tla mphemsa lefu	That will save me from death
Nyakallo ke e fumane	I have found joy
Tseleng ea hao Morena	In your ways Lord
Lira ho 'na li qhalane	My enemies have scattered
Ke hloletsoe ke uena	You won the fight for me
Ho tla ba joang ha ke siea	How will it be like when I leave
Kobo ena e bolang	This blanket that will decompose
Ke be joale ka Elia	And be like Elijah
Ka koloi e fofang?	With his flying motor
Ke tla opa ka liatla	I will clap my hands
Ke tla re: Alleluya	I will say Hallelujah
Alleluya ho senatla	Hallelujah to the hero
Se nkenyang ha Jehova!	That leads me to Jehova

* * *

These hymns are a connection to a time long gone, when the first converts embraced religion. They continue to echo in our churches almost two centuries later. It is in these hymns that we see a connection with the Kereke ya Fora. It's the same church founded by Casalis in Thaba Bosiu, where he and his brothers in Christ, Gosselin and Arbousset, worshipped with King Moshoeshoe.

Sitting with Takatso and mulling over these developments he cautioned: 'You can see that singing *Lifela tsa Sione* in the *Hosanna* was a political move. I was not there, but it was an obvious political ploy to hide something and to steal something. It must have been engineered from the NG Kerk, or mother church as they call it. I never got to ask Moruti Buti (father of Sam Buti) and Moruti Ntwane, who sat in those meetings to curate the *Hosanna* in Kroonstad, about the motive behind establishing the *Hosanna*.'

To many others who ended up in the NG Kerk and later URCSA they were reconnecting with the church brought by the French protestant missionaries. How the Boers got to take it and repackage it as a Boer daughter church is a matter to be investigated further, perhaps by students of theology or those interested in church history.

Takatso added: 'What I know is that the Boers came through Winburg and established their first church and they spread through the Orange Free State with their churches in the towns. The NG Kerk never intended to draw black people into the church. In 1853, the decision not to share the communion with other races, the African, Coloured and Khoisan, was taken by the Cape Synod. In the Free State, the NG Kerk never took that decision because they didn't share space with them anyway. The first Afrikaner church was built by Sir Harry Smith in Winburg, thanking the Boers for helping the Brits drive out amaXhosa across Fish River.

'The oldest NG Kerk in Afrika congregation in the Orange Free State is Brandfort, according to my research. The people know it as Kereke ya Fora. I called Moruti (Reverend) Nthakge to ask him how it was established. He said he never looked into it. He didn't know about Beersheba either. Even when we were in training in Turfloop, the White lecturers hid the story of Beersheba from us. I asked a missionary lecturer who taught at Unisa about the story of Beersheba later on and he said he knew about the massacre of black Christians there. He said there was a suspicion that those people would side with Moshoeshoe in the fight over the land of the Orange Free State.'

* * *

My own conclusion about the origins of Kereke ya Fora – taking in everything and knowing what I know now about the Beersheba Mission Station massacre of 1858 – is this: the Black church was appropriated by the NG Kerk without compensation either to the French or to Black Christians. Whether it was an amicable deal or daylight robbery, there was a take-over.

A historical note in the Reformed Family Forum website argues that NG Kerk ministers like Frazer of Phillippolis and Van der Wall of Bloemfontein objected strongly to the injustices done to the Paris Evangelical Mission Society (PEMS) in the wake of the Beersheba killings. The NG Kerk and the church in Lesotho nevertheless collaborated on and off throughout the 19th and 20th centuries, leading to the NG Kerk taking over some PEMS stations in the Orange Free State and supporting the PEMS work in Lesotho. The relationship broke down at the height of apartheid in the 1950s, only recovering as recently as 2008.

This is further evidence that the purported holy alliance between the White NG Kerk and the Black church of the French was founded on dubious blood-stained grounds.

I obtained my answer and established the French connection that has been troubling me for so long. I now know that the Black NG Kerk is rooted in the work of the French missionaries, and I should probably be kinder to my family for devoting so much of their time and effort to the church. For all intents and purposes, it did not start off as the apartheid church that it became known as for decades. Its creed and practices were hinged on the mission work of Casalis and Rolland. Kereke ya Fora is a church that was endorsed by the founding father of the Basotho nation, King Moshoeshoe I. And yes, the influence and power of the racist 'adoptive mother' NG Kerk gave it a notoriety it would battle to shake off.

However, I still have to reconcile with the decision Moshoeshoe made to give the French and Boers too much leeway to deculturalise his people. It was visionary of him to acknowledge the dawning of Western 'civilisation' here in southern Africa, and to call on the French missionaries to equip his people with the tools they needed, such as literacy and numeracy, to navigate a brave new world. But the cost has been high. African norms and traditions were undermined in favour of the White ways of doing things.

On the other hand, he trusted the Boers to roam unchecked until they became an unstoppable threat and for that I hold a dimmer view of him.

I can't help but wonder how this Christening project was implemented in the Basotho nation. Was there resistance? What happened to those who broke ranks? What became of centuries-old traditional belief systems? Were they discarded to the dustbin of culture and shunned without protest?

These are the frustrating questions those who are engaged with thinking about their identities in relation to history and ancestors consider. By what standards do we judge our forebears? We did not have their problems, their trust, their loyalties, their context. We can only measure them by the imperfect means of our own lens on life.

It is not easy to absolve the Black NG Kerk of its complicity in the painful legacy of its mother church. As Professor Tshepo Lephakga puts it, the church subscribed to separateness, oppression, humiliation and land dispossession that was later called apartheid. He blamed it on the misunderstanding and misinterpretation of the Bible and Calvinism. The grave consequences of the misguided philosophy have disadvantaged the majority of South

Africans who were pushed into the Bantustans. They left the country fragmented. The landless experienced a negative impact on their livelihood, psychology, economy and communal structures.

* * *

Lephakga argued that because of land dispossession, Blacks internalised oppression and doubted their humanness, fleeing from being Black. He put the blame at the door of the church and called for it to take responsibility in Black people reconciling with their humanity and attaining true reconciliation and true justice through land restitution.

Being landless and oppressed took so much away from Africans and the church didn't do much to alleviate their pain. Christianity purports to comfort the afflicted. Instead it added another layer to further dehumanise their African-ness and made of them imitations of the West, singing French hymns and classical compositions of Haydn instead of being allowed to express authentic and genuine African faith in the higher power.

I have to grapple with what it means to be a fourth-generation African Christian, to belong to a church my family gave its life to, and which lies at the heart of systematic racism in this country. This complex and problematic history is what has been bequeathed to me, and it sometimes leaves me riddled with angst.

But here I am now. What I choose is to embrace both my traditional heritage and the thorny religion I inherited. Thinking about these things gives me a better understanding of how I got here.

There is no denying that culture evolves and life changes, but the imperialisation and colonialism that followed the missionary work robbed Africans of what could potentially have been uniquely African, undiluted and genuine.

When it comes to the French missionaries, historian Robert July reminds us that at a time when Casalis et al embarked on their African expedition, French nationalism, that spiritual communion in the knowledge of the superiority of French civilisation, implied the obligation to share this greatness with other people. July says the aim was not only to colonise them, but also to teach them French culture and assimilate them into the French nation because they believed in the superiority of the French culture. It directed them to teach people to ignore and despise their own culture and history.

The missionary zeal of the British humanitarianism of the day may not have been as well developed among the French, but their feeling for cultural mission was clear and strong and far more self-conscious than with the English.

When you begin to understand how the French missionaries operated among their converts it is clear that, as July put it, humanitarianism from the times of Enlightenment was the belief in the goodness and perfectibility of man. They seem to have understood this through an appeal to the heart and spirit rather than rational thought. The 19th-century romantic impulses resulted in a religious revival in Europe of evangelical character and linked to this was a strong missionary movement designed to bring peoples in far-off parts of the world not only the comforts of Christianity, but the benefits of a 'higher' European civilisation.

July says in the 19th century the French sought to fulfil the humanitarian impulse by 'assisting' Africans in achieving a better life. However, the very idea of the helping hand implied a sense of cultural superiority and a humiliating unhumanitarian condescension.

The legacy of the missionaries remains problematic. As the academic and film producer Bhekizizwe Peterson argued, the appraisals have been divergent. On the one hand they have been hailed as harbingers of Western civilisation, while on the other they are held responsible for razing to the ground African social and cultural systems. In their wake was a new African, unrecognisable from his people. He spoke differently, behaved and dressed like a foreigner to them, and aspired to a world far removed from what they knew.

19
Is 'theft' the charge?

In rewriting and retelling our history, we find that it gets disputed and may cause conflict. I turned to my journalistic skills and offered a right of reply to the NG Kerk about what really happened in the wake of the Beersheba Massacre and how the Kereke ya Fora became known as NG Kerk in Afrika.

It seemed to me that Kereke ya Fora had been appropriated.

I reached out to Reverend Nelis Janse van Rensburg, the moderator based in Cape Town. He directed me to church historian Dr Gideon van der Watt, a senior theology lecturer at the University of the Free State in Bloemfontein. Van der Watt was prompt in his response when I emailed him my enquiry. In his reply, he pointed out that his account was off the cuff, yet his perspective was detailed and fascinating.

The 1858 attack on Beersheba, where innocent people were murdered for no reason in a shocking act of violence, brutality and disloyalty to ideals of humanism in any culture's definition, was, Van der Watt told me, a sad and indefensible event.

He stated that there were no apparent reasons for the attack. The people in the station were innocent. Missionary Rolland and the leaders (who were the chiefs) at the station had deliberately tried to stay neutral in the war between the Boers and Moshoeshoe.

They complied with the demands of the Boers, even though the demands were totally unjustified. History shows that Landdrost Sauer deceived them and acted mostly on the basis of his own greed – he personally stole the cattle and other belongings. He also deceived his own government – the then-president acknowledged that what had happened was wrong. Of course, this 'acknowledgement' was by far not enough to make retribution for the terrible deed.

Van der Watt said Reverend AA Louw, who was then the Moderator of the NG Kerk in the Orange Free State, and many members of the church, published an open letter of protest against what happened. But the Orange Free State Republic eventually doubled down on this injustice to the French mission stations when in the 1860s they banned missionaries from working in their stations within the area they called the 'conquered territory' west of the Caledon River.

Addressing my hypothesis that the White NG Kerk had 'stolen' the French church in the eastern Free State, Van der Watt charted a long history of cooperation between the two institutions.

He pointed out that despite the problematic and murderous past, the relationship between the PEMS missionaries and the NG Kerk in the Free State was restored in the 1870s. He said there were numerous examples of cooperation, mutual visits, official church relationships, joint conferences, sending of greetings at the respective synods, the mutual ordination of ministers, and financial contributions of the NG Kerk Free State to the PEMS work in Lesotho.

He noted that in 1887 several mission stations of the PEMS – like in Bethulie, Smithfield (Beersheba) and others in the eastern Orange Free State – were transferred to the NG Kerk Mission Church. This was officially done, he said, per agreement, so that PEMS could focus on Lesotho and some congregations in the Witwatersrand (today's Gauteng).

'I think it would be difficult to find historical evidence that the

NG Kerk "stole" it or forcefully took it from the PEMS. It was done after deliberations and mutual consent,' Van der Watt said, giving me a detailed explanation of relationships, timelines, geography and influences.

Van der Watt said a 'domestic mission' implemented in 1865, just seven years after the Beersheba Massacre, by the White NG Kerk sought to recruit Black members or Sesotho-speaking people to the church. Later on, specific missionaries and eventually Black evangelists focused on this work. These new congregations were duplicates of the White church following the same church order, worship service and theology, and they didn't allow for the integration of the Sesotho culture.

The Black church established in 1910 as the NG Kerk in Afrika borrowed from the older French sister church with some of its ministers trained in Morija at the seminary of the French Church. They sang the same hymns from *Lifela tsa Sione* and maintained a strong Reformed theological identity. The church in Lesotho and NG Kerk in Afrika kept a strong relationship and even attended each other's synods. A missionary from the Paris Evangelical Mission Society, who Van der Watt does not name, helped set up the NG Kerk in Afrika seminary in Lefika, Qwaqwa, and there are many documented examples of the closeness between the churches.

It was only in the early 1940s that an agreement was reached with PEMS that the NG Kerk would take care of the ministry of Lesotho migrant workers in the Orange Free State and Gauteng mines, while the PEMS would concentrate on Lesotho. The relationship unravelled in 1948, with the introduction of apartheid. The NG Kerk justified it on Biblical grounds and the Lesotho Evangelical Church of Southern Africa (LECSA) was critical. The earlier agreement was broken, and each started operating independently in each other's territory with limited success, which is why the NG Kerk in

Afrika is not a big church in Lesotho and LECSA, which grew out of the PEMS, is not big in South Africa.

The women's ministry uniforms of modern-day URCSA (top left and bottom right) and Fora ya Lesotho – literally translated as the Church of France in Lesotho as it is colloquially known and officially referred to as Lesotho Evangelical Church in Southern Africa or LECSA (top right and bottom left) – have an uncanny resemblance and point to the historical links explored in this book. PHOTO: AUTHOR/FACEBOOK

Will we ever really know the true origins of the Black arm of NG Kerk? Or are they lost in history and endlessly open to interpretation? And would knowing help me formulate a personal response?

So much of history has suffered at the hands of politics in this country. So many Black South Africans are disconnected from their histories and heritage, with so much having gone unrecorded or not archived or even having been actively suppressed.

Van der Watt lamented the break in the church. He himself has played a role in restoring the battered relationship between the NG Kerk mother church in the Free State, and the Lesotho Evangelical Church in Southern Africa. The relationship, he said, was now very warm.

'The very sad, unbiblical and sinful thing is that the Black church, from its very beginnings around 1865, developed separately from the White church. From the beginning the idea was to establish independent, separate, indigenous and so-called daughter churches – thus entrenching separateness (later on called apartheid).

'To this day, we are struggling desperately to reunite the separate NG Kerk churches. I gave my whole ministry of 40 years to this ideal ... but for various reasons we are now further apart than any time in history,' Van der Watt concluded.

Though church history is important for me in understanding my own story, all I know is that when I stand in church on a Sunday morning singing hymns by Samuel Rolland, Francois Coillard, Eugene Casalis and Thomas Arbousset that fill my body and my soul, I feel in my heart that Kereke ya Fora – the 'French' church – is connected by a golden thread to the great Moshoeshoe, who was hospitable to the French missionaries who entered his kingdom and who worked there.

* * *

It is an undeniable fact that this church of my grandfather has a complicated and painful past of violence, death, segregation and oppression. One cannot simply dismiss it though as the church of the Boers.

It is rooted in the work of the French Missionaries of the PEMS. Generations of Black Christians had the church of apartheid, the NG Kerk, imposed on them when, in fact, many African believers first heard the gospel and converted to the values of Christianity as preached by Samuel Rolland at Beersheba, and Casalis, Arbousset and Goselin in Thaba Bosiu, Morija and other stations.

The Boer influence and Afrikaans takeover is a point of contention and pain that our ancestors must have battled to reconcile. We, the later generations, have to defend ourselves when accused of belonging to a problematic church that justified apartheid.

But our membership of the NG Kerk was never a simple matter of choice.

The blood of the innocent Beersheba Christians cries for justice and it's our duty to tell their hidden and untold bloody story.

The relations go even further as Edwin Smith records that in 1848 the PEMS experienced a deficit, and to reduce expenditure the missionaries were directed to not open new stations and to sustain themselves with gardens and herds. Eugene Casalis was sent to visit the Dutch Reformed Churches of the Boers in the Cape Colony to solicit help.

20
We shall sing a new song

By the time of the Beersheba Mission Station attack, Samuel Rolland had already become a dominant figure in the eastern Orange Free State communities. He was called *Moruti* (Teacher) by all.

A biography found at Morija Museum and Archives, handwritten by an unknown author, provides some interesting insights about the missionary who – it might surprise him to know – came to be the ancestor of the NG Kerk in Africa, now known as the Uniting Reformed Church.

Rolland was born in 1801 in Neuchatel, Switzerland. Swept up by the spirit of le Réveil, a revival movement in the Swiss Reformed Church, he sailed down to what was then known as British Kaffraria to work for the Paris Evangelical Missionary Society (PEMS). France, being a Catholic state at that time, would not sponsor protestant missionaries, so he and his brothers in faith had to rely on the little they could scrape together in the name of mission work.

He was welcomed by Robert Moffat of the London Missionary Society at Kuruman in 1829, where he learned Serolong, a dialect of the Setswana language. Rolland then headed on to Mosega, near today's Zeerust, which the unidentified author of his biography described as the capital city of the Bahurutshe whose chief was Mokata.

Frustrated by the interference of Mzilikazi, the Rollands then moved to Motito, today known as Bothithong, some 60 kilometres from Kuruman, until they were invaded. Unable to set up a station among Batswana, in 1835 Rolland recruited a few Bahurutshe converts and travelled into today's Free State, settling in the eastern part to start Beersheba, near where the small town of Smithfield stands today.

Their trek to Beersheba was not without incident. At the overflowing Vaal River, the Rollands and their followers had to wait three weeks for the water to recede before it was safe for them to cross. The wagon carrying the luggage crossed first, with the Africans swimming beside the bullocks. The second wagon, carrying Elizabeth Rolland, Samuel's wife, and the couple's eight-month-old baby, was swept away and washed ashore hitting a willow root. They were rescued by some Bushmen who happened to be nearby.

Only in 1841, once settled in Beersheba, did Rolland finally unpack the wooden printing press he had brought to Kuruman from Europe. This piece of machinery played a significant role in the writing of indigenous literature. He began this language work by composing evening hymns for the schoolchildren who were in the care of his wife, Elizabeth.

The biographer noted that the hymns were so successful that, with the help of an unknown young Mosotho, Rolland printed a small collection of 28 hymns that he published a year later. This laid the foundation for what would become *Lifela tsa Sione* (Hymns of Zion).

Rolland composed more hymns and translated some books of the Bible, such as Genesis, Exodus and Isaiah, into Sesotho. He had already translated Job in 1839 and completed the rest of the Old Testament in 1843. With the aid of fellow Frenchmen, identified only as JR Casalis and Monsieur Ludorf, they started printing some parts of the Bible in 1845. He also published *Moboleli oa Litaba* newspapers in Beersheba in 1841.

Rolland gained the reputation of being the most productive and talented missionary. Francois Coillard composed most of the hymns in the *Lifela tsa Sione* hymnbook, followed by Rolland. In addition to being the minister in residence, Rolland was the temporal leader and served as a messenger for Moshoeshoe, who gave orders to the residents of the mission station through him, including the Boers who were passing through the eastern Free State at the height of the Great Trek.

The Boers called Rolland The President and his flock became known as MaRoellane (the people of Rolland). He was voted the president of the Conference Missionnaire (Missionary Conference) for 20 years by fellow French missionaries who belonged to the Paris Evangelical Mission Society (PEMS), which had stations across Lesotho.

Rolland ran the thriving Beersheba station until 1858 when the Boers demolished it during the first Free State–Basotho War.

In 1862, he settled in Poortje (which became known as the New Beersheba) where his son, Emile Rolland, came to help him with missionary work.

At the end of March 1866, he was evicted from Poortje by the Boers and fled to Aliwal North where he was to spend more than two years in exile. He settled in Hermon in 1869, where Emile and some of his flock from Beersheba had taken refuge. He died in Hermon, without ever returning to France.

* * *

Elizabeth Rolland had come to Cape Town from England, unmarried, to introduce the system of infant schools, before meeting and marrying Samuel in 1834. She died in Lesotho in 1901 aged 102. She was a pioneer of education at Beersheba contributing to the spread of literacy in young Christians. She told her life story in

The Recollections of Elizabeth Rolland (1803 to 1901) providing great insights of their work and life as first-generation missionaries. The Rollands had three children: Catherine, Elise and Emile.

The enduring imprint of Samuel Rolland's work is still evident in today's church and worship, almost 190 years later, and it has reached thousands far and wide. His hymns, and the particular way they were sung, resonated with Christians of that time and also of today. *seRoellane* (the Rolland way) is a practice and conduct to aspire to. Singing *seBersheeba* (the Beersheba way) is synonymous with reaching the deepest realms of faith and spirituality brought on by the sombre and melancholy singing of hymns composed by Rolland.

* * *

In the Uniting Reformed Church, the liturgy features the confessional hymn *Libe Li Teng* (We See Sins) and the benediction hymn *Mohau oa Morena Jesu* (The Grace of Lord Jesus). Both are Rolland compositions.

My grandfather Mongangane's most favourite hymn *Ho Rorisoe Rato Lena Le Re Kopantseng Hammoho* (Let Us Praise This Love That Brought Us Together) is also from Rolland's ink.

When singing or listening to Rolland-composed hymns like the hugely popular *Ke Na Le Molisa* (I Have a Shepherd), the mournful *Ntate Ha Ke Sa Sepela* (Father I Won't Wander), the celebratory *Rea U Boka Morena* (We Praise You Lord), the uplifting *Bokang Molimo oa Khanya* (Praise Be to the God of Light), the reassuring *Nyakallang Lefatsheng Lohle* (Rejoice the World Over) and the pensive and reflective *Jehova, Moren'a Rona* (Jehova, our Lord), one detects an emotional value and poetic beauty that only a master wordsmith could conjure up.

It is remarkable that the idiomatic quality typical of African languages was not lost.

Today's Christians have put their stamp on these hymns to a point that the meaning is hard to decipher. There is too much noise and accompaniment that dilutes the message. Singing *seBersheeba* means letting go of the bells and whistles, the robust drums and beats and the stomping of feet so popular in the Uniting Reformed Church. These hymns provide moments of introspection and reflection when Christians may ponder each word with great understanding and comprehension.

The culture of hymn singing persists. It is so entrenched in our lives that we often do it instinctively. It may be at a funeral, a wedding, a birthday party, a stokvel or a community gathering – chances are that there will be an opening hymn sung before a sermon or the welcoming remarks.

Hymns have driven the gospel music industry for decades. While there are new compositions surfacing every day, hymns remain the staple for the Christian music space. Careers of musicians such as Lebo Sekgobela, Winnie Mashaba, Joyous Celebration ensemble and Solly Moholo stand on hymns that were composed almost 190 years ago by White French missionaries. The creativity of today's singers finds expression through these praise songs, adding elements to modernise the sound and tune, and making them dynamic, energetic and rousing.

There is something nostalgic, comforting, reassuring and warm about hymns. They trigger memories and feelings from people's childhood, whether at Sunday School, or at a church service on the lap of a mother or grandmother. What stays is a parent's favourite hymn, or a hymn that was sung on the day of a particularly memorable sermon. Hymns can make tears flow, emotions rise, memories gush. You can get swept up when a hymn is sung.

Singing hymns combines three experiences that can lead to a feeling of transcendence: shared religion, meditation and community singing. No wonder it is such a powerful social glue.

The work of Gerrit Jordaan is particularly interesting to me in understanding how hymns play such a central role in the life of an African Christian.

He makes some fascinating observations about hymn singing, which he calls the earliest examples where two diverse cultures met in South Africa. Hymns are an imported cultural object from Europe but a personal experience for an African, and an opportunity to create a new style that a congregation may identify with more directly. They are a matter of claiming an identity; they are cultural affirmation.

By 'giving' the Western style of singing that the missionaries taught and prescribed, they took something away from their converts. By adapting these hymns, people have found that thing again.

For me, this speaks to asserting the African identity on what was essentially a European exercise. The inspiration for *Lifela tsa Sione*, the first published hymnal by the French missionaries among Basotho, comes from the Swiss César Malan's compositions of 1700. Missionaries such as Rolland saw the importance of using hymn singing as the most effective method of attracting the attention of potential converts.

Jordan says the emphasis in the hymns started with the words and that the music was incidental. A few tunes were used interchangeably with different sets of lyrics. Eugene Casalis wrote in October 1833, four months after his arrival in Lesotho, that the hymns they taught 'made the truths of Christianity enter the souls [of the Basotho]'.

When they imposed their Western hymn-singing methods, the missionaries failed to harness the African elements. The robustness of the singing and ebullient nature of African traditional singing were dismissed since they viewed African music as heathen, nonsensical and barbaric.

They introduced four-part singing in a regular metre. Drum accompaniment was forbidden, and the congregation had to stand still when singing. The hymns were strophic and required definite beginnings and ends, in contrast to the antiphonal, circular structure in traditional South African singing practice. This is what *seBeersheba* singing would sound like: morose, pensive and even tortured.

The converts were eager to please their teachers and, probably out of a desire to be like them, took to the new singing prescripts. The missionary Daumas, in an 1847 letter, told of how well the European hymns had been accepted by Basotho. 'This music, grave and simple,' he wrote, 'was very quickly seized by the [Basotho], to whom it appealed very much; young and old sing it with the same joy.'

These new Africans that the missionaries carved out would be at odds with their foundations. They became alienated if not unrecognisable to their ilk. The new Western styles had a profoundly negative and lasting impact on traditional music practice.

Jordaan cites Hugh Tracey, the English ethnomusicologist who worked in central and southern African communities recording their traditional music. He wrote, in 1954, 'Once the floodgates of Western and other foreign intrusions had been opened, there was immediate change for the worse. The African's whole culture was exposed and vulnerable to attack by determined proselytisers, both progressists and priests, sinner and saint go hand in hand to destroy a continent's taste in music, and the victim heartily enjoys his new love songs and a shuffling of the feet in the hymns not written into the original text.'

The proliferation of foreign styles wiped out original forms of music and dancing and the indigenous arts lost both meaning and their role in social integration.

Researchers point to the fact that some of the Africans actually attempted to put their signature on these Western hymns. A letter authored by missionary Francois Maeder in 1841 explains how Basotho made some changes to European hymns. To his ear, this was a discord. He complained that the Basotho didn't know how to sing semitones and as such 'the melody lost its beauty and harmony', and that as soon as they learned a new song, they changed it, and it became unrecognisable. He did, however, compliment the converts for having a taste for song and for learning the tunes easily.

Maeder's complaint is a manifestation of African converts asserting their identity on a Western import. Their inclination when it came to singing directed them towards a different way to what the missionaries had anticipated. They couldn't help but employ what came naturally to them.

Lifela tsa Sione, originally titled *Lipesaleme e Lifela tsa Sione*, was written wholly in Sesotho and was initially published by the Paris Evangelical Missionary Society in 1854. It was the first hymnal in an indigenous South African language. Some 6 000 copies were printed, and they sold out in two months. Another 6 000 were printed and again sold out in two months. The next order was 3 600. The hymnal took a new name as *Lifela tsa Sione le tsa Bojaki* in 1892. The current print run dates to 2018.

The appetite for Sesotho hymns has remained consistent and the influence of *Lifela tsa Sione* is undeniable, supported by the southern African commonality of languages. Jordan found the hymnal used in a church in a Setswana-speaking North West town and, when he enquired why they would use a Sesotho hymnal, the answer was that Sesotho was regarded as a language of religion.

It is not unusual to find Setswana and Sepedi speakers who switch to Sesotho when they pray or preach. It happens almost automatically, and then Sesotho switches off once the sermon is finished and the last Amen is uttered.

This speaks to the power and influence of Sesotho, which had an early start in the faith communities of Lesotho and South Africa. When people migrated from the rural areas to towns and cities, they carried with them the practices of their religion and further spread them in bigger urban communities.

In the book *An introduction to the Music of Basotho*, music ethnologist Robin Wells argues that in the early 20th century Christianity spread rapidly in Lesotho and the hymns of the missionaries took over as the primary expression of religious identity.

An indication of the importance of hymn singing in the evangelisation project is that the missionaries Casalis and Rolland translated and published the New Testament a year after publishing *Lifela tsa Sione*. They completed the Bible only in 1881 (as mentioned earlier, Rolland started some of the books of the Bible in the 1840s). It is probably because of the Africans' affinity for singing as a cultural expression and a daily activity that composing indigenous hymns ranked higher than translating the Bible itself.

Lifela tsa Sione is printed in two versions: one for congregational use, containing only the text, and the other a version for choir containing four-part settings in tonic sol-fa, the system of naming the notes of the scale, which is used to teach singing.

Jordaan concludes that many of the hymns are not sung as they first were in the 1830s and 1840s.

* * *

Out of the 449 hymns in *Lifela tsa Sione*, only three are composed by Africans. *Molimo ke Moea* (God is a Spirit), hymn 445, is by the celebrated Sesotho composer Polumo Mohapeloa. The hymn is somewhat of a choral composition that sits comfortably in the Western singing tradition.

There is also *Ke Lesitsi, Ke Tla Feela* (I'm Mournful, I Come Empty), hymn 96, credited to Filemone Rapetloane, a literary pioneer who at some point edited *Leselinyana la Lesotho* newspaper, founded by Adolphe Mabille. He died in 1869.

The third hymn *Bolelang Taba Tsa Jesu* (Tell the News of Jesus), hymn 272, is recorded as composed by A Sello, but not much is known about him.

Some of the hymns in *Lifela tsa Sione* have been translated to other languages. Take for example the hit song *Ndezel' Uncedo* by Joyous Celebration, which attracted millions of views on YouTube within weeks. It was originally written by Samuel Rolland as the hauntingly mournful *Lala Ho Nna*. It has become popular in the Methodist church too, sung in isiXhosa with big energy and celebration.

The isiZulu hymnal *Amagama Okuhlabelela (Dumisane)* was published by the Anglican American Zulu Mission in 1850, making it the second indigenous collection of hymns to be created. The Setswana hymnal *Lifela tsa Sione tsa Tirelo (Kopelo)* was published by the Religious Tract Society in 1907, and the *Hosanna* was published in 1946 by the Dutch Reformed Church. In 1968, NG Kerk in Afrika published the *Hosanna* in isiZulu, isiXhosa, Sesotho and TshiVenda.

* * *

Perhaps it's time for Africans to sing a new song, composed by them and telling of their own Christian journey and experience. In the *Hosanna* of the NG Kerk in Afrika, more African composers are included and more global classical composers like Handel, Haydn and Beethoven. The challenge to build on hymns that have been sung by Africans for almost two centuries, and to inject them with the African aesthetic, perspective and energy, requires a shift in the mind of the singers to accept that their faith is yet to speak to the God of African ancestors.

21

Shaking mountains for answers

The author on top of Thaba Bosiu.

Thaba Bosiu, Lesotho, July 2022

Thaba Bosiu holds the honour of being the spiritual home of Basotho.

Writing this book gave me the opportunity to retell my story as a Mosotho man. And to do that, I needed to go to Lesotho so that I could see myself through the lens of the place to better understand my being, and how Western religion came to be so central to my family's life.

It was Thaba Bosiu I needed to get to.

It was here, in Maseru district, that the founder of the Basotho nation, King Moshoeshoe arrived at night from Botha-Bothe. He named the mountain he found there Thaba Bosiu – 'mountain at night'.

Legends abound about this mountain that became Moshoeshoe's fortress and stronghold. It is believed that it grows bigger at night or that it moves, and that if you took some sand away from it, the sand would disappear overnight to return to the mountain.

Practically speaking, it was strategically placed, making it safe and secure for the king – who occupied it in 1824 – and impenetrable for the enemy at a time of instability and war.

It was at Thaba Bosiu that the first French missionaries Eugene Casalis, Thomas Arbousett and Constand Gosselin arrived in 1833. They we were welcomed by Ramatseatsana 'Mote who had settled at the foot of the mountain with his family. A day or two later, they went up the mountain to meet Moshoeshoe.

Two things make Thaba Bosiu such a profoundly important place when one speaks about the Basotho nation. It is here that the Basotho were formed as a people, and it is here that Christianity was rooted.

The trajectory of Basotho took a different course as Christianity infiltrated every aspect of their existence. The missionaries set out to introduce Western values and practices that often clashed with African practices like mahadi (or lobola, as it is known in other languages) and polygamy. From the contact between the Europeans and the Basotho, a new generation emerged, one that could read and write. By 1863, a mere 30 years after the first missionaries arrived at Thaba Bosiu, a newspaper titled *Leselinyana la Lesotho* was started by Adolphe Mabille produced in Morija, a town fondly known as *Letsha la Thuto* (the well of education). It was widely read by the literate beneficiaries of mission education. Earlier, there was also *Moboleli oa Litaba*, a newspaper produced in Beersheba, in present-day eastern Free State, by missionary Samuel Rolland in the 1850s, which is possibly the oldest serial publication aimed at the literate Black readers in this part of the world.

After the destruction of Beersheba, it was from Morija, not far from Maseru in western Lesotho, that the printing of newspapers, pamphlets, books and flyers flourished. One can safely say that Morija took Sesotho to the world. Today, Sesotho may have numerically fewer speakers than most languages, but the prestige and power of the language of Basotho remain unassailable in the realm of religious worship.

It was also in Morija that the iconic *Lifela tsa Sione* was produced. This collection of hymns composed and recorded in Sesotho by the missionaries with the aid of their Black understudies continues to be a permanent fixture in the lives of thousands of people who live nowhere near Morija. These hymns were translated into other languages and have been sung in isiZulu, isiXhosa, Tshivenda, Xitsonga, Siswati, Setswana and Sepedi.

* * *

These are the days, finally, of Black people reclaiming their stories and histories and re-imagining their positions in a society that has been forcibly shaped around the ideas of Europeans, ideas they spread, often violently, in great swathes across the African continent and elsewhere.

As a practising Black Christian man, I needed to understand my own position in the world too. My people have always been church people. My great-grandfather was an elder in the African Methodist

Episcopal Church. My grandfather was an evangelist of the Dutch Reformed Church. My late father was an elder, one uncle is a retired minister, another a retired evangelist, and so many other uncles were elders. Going to church is a non-negotiable in my family. Our children are baptised and have been brought up in the church.

Church is central to our existence and that's been the case for over 100 years.

I headed to Lesotho to shake the mountains for answers about what all of this means to me, now, here. I had to retrace the steps of my forebears. As somebody who grew up so far away from the land of my ancestors, it was going to be too much to take in when the moment of reckoning arrived.

* * *

It was an early morning ascension up Thaba Bosiu. Energetic, full of life and filled with anticipation, I sprinted up 600 metres, give or take, to the summit with ease. I had a guide with me, a kind young man named Lebohang Mafa, but I had no idea what to expect from my reaction to the place.

The flat-topped mountain has seven passes including Khubelu, Ramaseli, Mokhachane and Makara.

The sweeping views of Thaba Bosiu extend for dozens of kilometres. As I sat on the boulder that is known as Moshoeshoe's chair, I felt history so close to me I could touch it. I *was* touching it.

It was from this vantage point that I, like Moshoeshoe did some 200 years ago, took in unfettered views of the plains, the ridges and crevices of the mountains, and rivers. This is where Moshoeshoe used to sit and survey his kingdom.

Nothing could have prepared me for the swelling of emotions as I stood by the grave of Moshoeshoe on Thaba Bosiu. His final resting place is marked by a neat arrangement of stones. The simple headstone is inscribed 'Morena Moshoeshoe I'.

I bowed my head in prayer and felt an overwhelming sense of connection with my identity.

This is where a man I was taught about in school, and whose name is etched in the history of African history, rested.

The stories are endless; the legend is larger than life. His power, prowess and intelligence have been the cornerstone of Basotho identity. They are not called the people of love and peace for nothing: this is what Moshoeshoe's quiet diplomacy advocated.

And here I stood at the grave of the father of Bashoeshoe, as Basotho are sometimes referred to. It felt like I was there to represent all the Mofokengs who could not be there with me: my late grandparents, my father Moses, my mother, my entire family.

All of us there – in the simple form of one man trying to find the path that brought him to the middle of his life and who wondered where it would take him next – came together that day to pay respects to this great ancestor of a nation we belong to.

* * *

Nearby, is the tomb of King Moshoeshoe II. A granite monstrosity that reflects modern tastes. The contrast between the two is telling.

King Moshoeshoe I died in 1870. King Moshoeshoe II in 1996. Two generations of Basotho rulers are separated by a century of upheaval and by the small distance between their final resting places. One is marked by a heap of rocks, symbolising oneness with the earth. The other is shiny and palatial and is surrounded by palisade fencing. The differences are striking. How much has changed since Basotho became a nation.

Standing at the tomb of King Moshoeshoe I on top of Thaba Bosiu.

There are a few other graves of Basotho chiefs and headmen (and women) that surround the graves of the two kings. Walking around here truly brings the expression 'walking among greats' to life.

It is customary to wash one's hands after standing at the grave, so I walked over to *seliba sa 'MaMohato* (the well of 'MaMohato). Moshoeshoe had over 150 wives. 'MaMohato was the principal wife, effectively the mother of the Basotho nation. Where I am washing my hands is from the well that she used. It is one of eight springs found on Thaba Bosiu.

As I gulped the sweet and cool waters from the spring, brought to my mouth with the cup of my hands, my guide told me that this wasn't just any water, that it carried spiritual and healing qualities. I used the moment again to connect, saying silent prayers and asking for the blessings of my ancestors. As the water ran down my throat into my body, I felt a shift.

Drinking from *seliba sa 'MaMohato*.

This was probably one of the most peaceful states I had ever experienced. The sense of protection and comfort, like I had reunited with my favourite blanket from when I was a child. I felt cradled, heard, seen and appreciated by my ancestors.

It is hard to describe what happens when you go through such an out-of-body experience, but all I can tell you, with great humility, is that I felt it.

When I stood up from the spring, I felt fortified. I had drunk from the well of my grandmothers. I was in communion with my ancestors.

The guide said that this well was one of the best kept secrets in Lesotho. People travelled from as far as India and the Americas to drink from this spring, he told me. Some of them have told him that they had visions to travel to Lesotho in order to find *seliba sa 'MaMohato* and to drink from it. They reported having been healed of their ailments, and those who needed clarity of thought and guidance left with contentment and peace. Many more Basotho would rather go to *seliba sa 'MaMohato* and drink from there than to fill two-litre bottles with sea water from Durban or Cape Town in search of answers for life's trouble.

* * *

The guide and I took a turn to the west and ended up at the ruins of 'MaMohato's house.

The walls are still standing but the roofs are gone. It is part of the four-house royal compound where remnants of a community of old remain. Further on is the abode of King Moshoeshoe I. It's a rectangular stone house built in 1837 by Private David Webber from the Seaforth Highlanders who was given sanctuary by Moshoeshoe while fleeing from enemies. He was a mason and a carpenter, and he constructed the two-roomed house with modern sensibilities.

I went through the door, and I touched the walls. There's not much left except the walls. The floor is sandy, interspersed sporadically with tufts of grass. When I noticed pieces of paper strewn on the ground, I complained to the guide about the littering. To my eyes this was sacrilegious and a desecration of a holy ground. The guide, however, told me that these were letters to the father of Basotho. They were penned by people from all over the world expressing their wishes and giving blessings. Some of them were asking for health, marriage and long life, others for children or cars, still others were expressing a wish to win the Lotto or Powerball.

* * *

To the east of Thaba Bosiu lies a curious mountain. Its shape is recognisable in the *mokorotlo*, the Basotho straw hat. It is called Qiloane, a Khoisan name. This was the name of mount Thaba Bosiu before Moshoeshoe renamed it 'mountain at night'.

The symbolism and the iconography of the land and what they represent to Basotho make Thaba Bosiu a magical place.

The evidence of a communal life on Thaba Bosiu remains. The ruins, foundations, trees, paths and collections of rocks tell of a people who were mighty and powerful. People on whose shoulders and backs I stand.

The air is crisp and light, and the grass is tall and moist from the early morning dew. I belong to Bafokeng, the people of the dew.

* * *

Coming down from Thaba Bosiu, I felt in the depth of my soul that I had been in communion with my forebears. The remarkable experience of vising Thaba Bosiu, of being that close to history, filled me with optimism for tomorrow. We are part of a chain that can never be broken. We owe it to our ancestors to tell their stories and to make them proud with the opportunities we now enjoy.

I'm not one prone to headaches, but when I descended Thaba Bosiu I had a pounding one that lasted two days.

I let the body heal itself after this spiritual encounter.

* * *

It is said that King Moshoeshoe descended from Thaba Bosiu every Sunday morning for a church service with the missionaries on the grounds of what is now known as Lesotho Evangelical Church of Southern Africa (LECSA). Back then, in the 1830s, it was the gathering place of early Christians who listened to the Word and worshipped together, led by the founding fathers of the Basotho nation, Moshoeshoe and his council of elders and chiefs, who were so hospitable to the European missionaries and who welcomed Christianity. It's probably here that the first hymns were sung, and the first baptisms took place. The conversion to Christianity quickened its pace at the cradle of a nation.

Surrounded by mountain ranges and with the Phutiatsana river that runs through it, Thaba Bosiu is picturesque. The gorges, valleys and ridges are part of its natural rugged beauty.

A few steps from the church, the new Heroes' Acre is under construction. A curious tombstone caught my eye. It's the resting place of Tsepo Tshola, fondly known as the Village Pope. In my many years as a journalist, I had the pleasure of meeting and interviewing Ntate Tshola several times. We established that we have family links. His father and my mother's uncle, Tsepo Masithela, were both ministers of the AME church and had been good friends. The relationship went so deep that when Tshola senior had his son, he named him after Tsepo Masithela. Whenever I met Ntate Tshola he always reminded me that he was the first grandson of the Masithela family.

Standing at his tomb on what was incidentally the first anniversary of his death during this meaningful pilgrimage for me was a fate only God and the ancestors could have conjured.

* * *

There is an imposing boulder that sits curiously in one of the yards in Thaba Bosiu. It looks like it rolled down the mountain apocalyptically and settled on the flat ground among the villagers. One wonders what it might have destroyed or flattened in its wake.

The closer you get to it, the more fully you fathom its largeness. It is two times taller than an average human and is probably about ten metres wide. It is known as the Ramatseatsana rock. It is exactly here, in June 1833, that the French missionaries reported themselves and met the owner of the house Ramatseatsana 'Mote who would introduce them to Moshoeshoe. The descendants of the 'Mote still live in the house and are aware of the historical significance of their home. The Ramatseatsana Award is a national order bestowed on outstanding Basotho by King Letsie II and is named after their great-great-great-grandfather. He was the first convert in Lesotho.

In front of the Ramatseatsana boulder where the first missionaries arrived in 1833.

Pope John Paul II came to Lesotho in the 1980s. An outdoor stage stands in memory of him, entirely intact, as it would have been when the Pope stood there at the place where Christianity was first introduced to the area. There is a photograph of him wearing a hat in the shape of Qiloane and a Basotho blanket.

Attached to the main building of the church is a curious little room that is kept under lock and key. It is a sacred space, rarefied like the chapels of the Vatican City, except this is a modest room decorated with the finest Basotho *litema* (wall decorations). It retains the authenticity of the time of Moshoeshoe. A traditional broom is kept in here. My assumption was that the broom was both symbolic and practical. On the one hand, the broom keeps the house of the king clean in all senses, especially spiritually, and it is an artefact from his time. On the other, it would be sacrilege to use the same broom used all over the church in this holiest of holy places, so they kept a special one for use in the special room.

This is where Moshoeshoe's 'chair' is kept. This is the rock upon which Moshoeshoe sat during church services with the French missionaries, and here it is, 200 years later. A painting of an older Moshoeshoe is kept in the sacred room too.

While the church building is not the actual one that the French missionaries constructed, the spiritual connection remains.

* * *

The trees around the area tell a story not dissimilar to the story of humans. There is an oak tree, which is not indigenous to Lesotho, and several other plants that were brought over by the missionaries and are now scattered in the yards of Basotho in Thaba Bosiu. They stay. They grow. They become a part of the landscape, whether they belong, in the strictest sense, or not.

The Basotho Cultural Village down the road from the church attracts tourists from around the world. The tourism authorities of Lesotho recognise the value that Thaba Bosiu can bring to the country's gross domestic product. Here, they tell the story of the Basotho nation using the different clans and their totems. The village is located at the foot of Thaba Bosiu and it takes a few steps to get you on one of the passes that will take you up to the summit.

That was the summit I climbed on that day, but I had long been ascending the path towards better understanding of myself and my family, and the mountains that I needed to shake for our story to come rolling out.

After Thaba Bosiu, my soul was fulfilled, my spirit revived and my vision was cleared.

It may be a 'mountain at night', but this visit brought so much light into my life.

Born hundreds of kilometres from Lesotho and brought up to be proud of my Sesotho language and culture, even when surrounded by people of a different persuasion, practices and beliefs, I needed to stand at the grave of King Moshoeshoe I to declare the ways in which we had kept the faith.

On behalf of my grandparents and parents I raised my hand and connected with a past we could never touch. All we could do was to imagine our history.

I went up Thaba Bosiu not only to walk among giants but to touch history.

Acknowledgements

I have always been something of a curiosity when topics of religion and church come up, and the fact that I attend the NG Kerk tends to elicit gasps of disbelief and stares. I never thought much of the church I grew up in, the one my grandfather gave 32 years of his life as an evangelist. My father and my uncles were all elders and deacons, and one of them became an evangelist and another a minister. We have always been *batho ba kereke ya Fora* (people of the Church of France) as NG Kerk is known in African communities, but we never spoke French, it was Afrikaans instead. All the church magazines, documents and communication were in Afrikaans with a Sesotho translation. My grandfather was fluent in Afrikaans and was the *tolk* (interpreter) whenever an Afrikaans minister climbed into the pulpit. This idea of being odd got me to question my identity and set me on a path to understand my forebears better.

I wish to thank the 2019/20 Masters long form/narrative journalism class at the University of the Witwatersrand, Johannesburg, for encouraging me to explore this curiosity. In particular, I must thank my supervisor Kevin Davie, who helped me craft my dissertation, the book form of which you now hold in your hands. Special thanks are due to the course coordinator Professor Lesley Cowling whose insights and words of encouragement kept me going until the end, and my classmate Lebogang Seale for his support during the many hours we spent on our research projects during the difficult times of the Covid-19 pandemic.

This quote by Barbara J Starmans, published on The Social Historian website, succinctly explains why we do what we do: 'We study the past even as we live in the present and we struggle to imagine what it was like when our ancestors walked the earth.'

History has been my interest since my school days at ZM Seatlholo High School in Lotlhakane village, Mafikeng under the tutelage of Mr Amos Lesetedi, the one teacher who had the most impact on my young mind. I wish to acknowledge his influence here. And thank you Mme Shirley Lebotse for the support towards my studies.

Starmans further challenges us to ponder over these words: 'What is the present for us, was the future for our ancestors, and what is the past for us was the present for our ancestors. Our present will be the past of the generations who come after us.'

We are part of a continuum. A chain that stretches back many centuries. We are not rootless beings with no past. Our past doesn't start at apartheid, it goes beyond it. It is a thousand years deep. We have to make that link. We have to dig deep to establish the connection with our ancestors.

I'm also inspired by this quote from @melanated_facts on Instagram: 'Africans must know their own history, for it is needed to correctly read the language of their own ancestors.'

Our ancestors continue to speak to us, but we can't hear them because we are so far removed from the world they inhabited. Even the language we use is so foreign that we fail to see the signs and hear their whispers and faint murmurings echoing from centuries ago.

My deepest gratitude goes to my children, Mahali Leseli and Chapatso Kgosi Mofokeng, who stood by me during the research of this book. We travelled together across Free State, North West, Gauteng and Lesotho, and their patience with me was remarkable.

This book was written in Johannesburg, Mafikeng, Maseru, Morija, Thaba Bosiu, Paris and Nancy, and was a collaborative effort with scholars, academics, family and friends.

My uncle Professor Takatso Mofokeng's generosity in sharing his knowledge, notes and insights challenged my thinking and got me here. Thank you for the time you set aside in Devon and in Henley-on-Klip to share your wisdom with me, to assist me and to tell me the story of your father, Mongangane Mofokeng, and the church he served so diligently.

I wish to acknowledge my cousin Limpho Masithela who took me to Thaba Bosiu and insisted that this was an important aspect of my research. At that time, I had set my heart on Morija and Maseru only. She made sure that I went to Thaba Bosiu, and there I had the most spiritually fulfilling and uplifting experience of my life. It breaks my heart that Limpho was brutally killed, allegedly by her lover, just a week after I returned from Thaba Bosiu. Rest in peace Mokoena, and thank you for the contribution you made to this study.

Ntate Stephen Gill, aka Teboho Morejele, at Morija Museum and Archives, and your colleagues Matseliso Phethoka and Liako Mahao, thank you for your patience and assistance during my time in Lesotho.

Lebohang Mafa, the guide who took me up to the summit of Thaba Bosiu and guided me as I reconnected with my past, thank you.

I acknowledge the contribution of Professor Jacob Dlamini (Princeton University) and Professor Gilbert Motsaathebe (North West University) for the improvements you suggested for this manuscript and for weighing in on my earlier efforts.

Bongani Madondo and Zandle Sebona, thank you for your valuable input when I started writing this manuscript.

Thank you to my French academic family, Professor John Bak of University de Lorraine, and Professor Gilles Tiulies of Aix-Marseille University, for your perspectives. Thank you to my friend Indiana Lods from University of Burgundy in Dijon, who assisted me with translations from French to English.

It would be remiss not to acknowledge the support of Ntate Tebogo Seokolo, South Africa's ambassador to France and his wife Moipone, who welcomed me in their home when I was conducting research for this book in Paris. What was supposed to be a 30-minute meet-and-greet, became a three-hour conversation on history, politics and life. Thank you David Tlale for the introduction.

Thank you to my colleagues at the Lesotho Research Group at the University of Cape Town for always deepening my understanding of the history of Lesotho, and for the access you provided to some of the rare publications that I quote in the book.

Thank you to my spiritual home, Uniting Reformed Church (URCSA) in Alexandra, particularly the support and prayers of my brethren Malebana Boshomane (my elder), Thabang Tsautse, Thapelo Molekwa, Phillip Kanyane, and all the members of my beloved Christian Men's Ministry (CMM). A special mention of the members of my Ward 13 and the extended Johannesburg Presbytery. My brethren at Methodist Church in Alexandra's Young Men's Guild (YMG), particularly brother Tsietsi Madibo and brother Stephens Pelo, thank you.

Thank you to my friends and family: my mother Lebohang Mofokeng (and the Masithela family); my brother Thabiso Mofokeng; my sister Palesa Mofokeng; my aunts and uncles, cousins, nephews and nieces; and my people Elias Lempe, Hloni Modise, Max Mmethi, Emmanuel Tjiya, Moipone Malefane, Paledi Segapo, Molato Phakwago, Sdu Gerasch, Tlaleng Mofokeng,

Adv. Nkateko Maluleke, Lionel Jamela, Abram Sokupha, Danny Baloyi, Dollar Manyaapelo, Mongameli Tyamzashe, Thabang Mokopanele, Lerato Matsoso, Lucas Mahlakgane, Lerato Molete, Maseipati Tsotsotso, Happy Ngidi, Elizabeth Sejake, Louise Pillay, Kentridge Tlale, Germina Shashape, Mathoto Mathopa, Susan Radebe, Lerato Tlhakwana, Mapitsi Manabile and Fezile Makhanya; and the Masithela family in Gauteng, Lesotho, Free State and Northern Cape.

Thank you to my colleagues at the Recording Industry of South Africa (RiSA), especially my boss, Advocate Nhlanhla Sibisi, for their unwavering support.

To my cheerleaders, and there are many, across social media and in the real streets, thank you for your support and love.

I wish to mention Daniel Pooe, the most diligent and hardest working man at Postnet Meyersdal for always going the extra mile with my requests and print orders.

I owe a debt of gratitude to Karin Schimke, the editor of this book. She was thorough, patient and understanding in bringing out the best of me in this work. It was a joy to work with you in crafting a book I am sure we are all proud of.

To the most patient, kind and supportive publisher Gill Moodie, thank you. You gave me more than enough time to work on my manuscript and allowed me space to create what I wanted. You encouraged me when I felt I couldn't write anymore. I hope I make you proud.

And finally, to God, our father, the Creator of the heavens and earth. All glory and praise to Him.

This book is a celebration of the memory of my late grandparents, Mongangane Wilfred Mofokeng and Mahadi Maria Mofokeng, and my father, Moses Teboho Mofokeng.

Bibliography

Books and articles

Bac, M. (1985) *Progress Towards Health For All in the Gelukspan Health Ward.* Medunsa.

Boesak, A. (1984) *Black and Reformed: Apartheid, Liberation and Calvinist Theology.* Skotaville.

Bonner, P and Nieftagodien, N. (2008) *Alexandra: A history.* Wits University Press.

Bonner, P; Nieftagodien, N and Mathabatha, S. (2012) *Ekurhuleni: The making of an urban region.* Wits University Press.

Bredekamp, H and Ross, R. (1995) *Missions and Christianity in South African History.* Wits University Press.

Casalis, E. (1861) *The Basutos.* James Nisbet & Co.

Cole, E. (1967) *House of Bondage.* Random House

Coplan, D. (1994) *In the Time of Cannibals: The Word Music of South Africa's Basotho Migrants.* University of Chicago Press.

Coplan, D. (2009) *Erasing History: The Destruction of the Beersheba and Platberg African Christian Communities in the Eastern Orange Free State, 1858–1983.* Taylor & Francis.

Crais, C and McClendon T., editors. (2014) *The South Africa Reader – history, culture, politics.* Duke University Press.

Dlamini, J. (2020) *The Terrorist Album.* Harvard University Press.

Edgar, R. (1982) *The International Journal of African Historical Studies*, Vol. 15, No. 3. Boston University African Studies Center.

Ellenberger F. (1997) *History of Basuto, Ancient and Modern*. Morija Museum & Archives.

Fanon, F. (1952) *Black Skin, White Masks*. Pluto Press.

Fanon, F. (1963) *The Wretched of the Earth*. Grove Weidenfeld, New York.

Fanon, F. (1964) *Toward The African Revolution*. Grove Press.

French, K. (1983) *James Mpanza and the Sofasonke Party in the Development of Local Politics in Soweto*. University of the Witwatersrand.

Frescura, F. (2015) 'A Case of Hopeless Failure: The Role of Missionaries in the Transformation of Southern Africa's Indigenous Architecture'. Journal for the Study of Religion, Vol. 28, No. 2.

Futhwa, F. (2012) *Bafokeng*. Nalane.

Gill, S. (1993) *A Short History of Lesotho*. Morija Museum & Archives.

Isichei, E. (1995) *A History of Christianity in Africa*. SPCK.

Jordaan, G. (2013) *Hymn Singing in Sesotho/Setswana/Sepedi churches: a process of claiming and reclaiming*. Muziki.

Julian, J. (1892) *Dictionary of Hymnology*. Charles Scribner's Sons.

July, R. (1968) *The Origins of Modern African Thought*. Faber and Faber Ltd.

Khati, T. (2015) *Missionary Work in Africa in Eugene Casalis's Time and Beyond*. Cambridge Scholars Publishing.

Kirk, JA. (2000) *What is Mission? Theological Explorations*. Augsburg: Fortress.

Korf, L. (2007) *Podium and/or Pulpit?* Historia.

Kritzinger, JNJ. (1988) *Black Theology – Challenge to Mission*. University of South Africa.

Kritzinger, JNJ. (2008) *Starting From Stofberg – A Brief Survey of Hundred Years of Missionary Theological Education in the DRC family 1908–2008.*

Landau, P. (2010) *Popular Politics in the History of South Africa, 1400–1948.* Cambridge University Press.

Lelyveld, J. (1982) *The Life and Death of a Nonconformist Afrikaner.* The New York Times.

Lephakga, T. (2014) *The History of Theologised Politics of South Africa, the 1913 Act and Its Impact on the Flight from the Black Self.* UNISA.

Letsosa, R and De Klerk, B. (2007) *A Relevant Liturgy for Reformed Churches of African Origin Concerning Liturgical Music.* North West University.

Leshota, P. (2014) *Postcolonial Reading of Nineteenth-Century Missionaries' Musical Texts: The Case of Lifela tsa Sione and Lifela tsa Bakritse.* Taylor & Francis.

Machobane, B. (2001) *Essays on Religion and Culture Among Basotho.* Mazenod Publishers.

Maguire, R. (1991) *The Peoples' Club: A social and institutional history of Orlando Pirates Football Club, 1937–1973.* University of the Witwatersrand.

Mandela, N. (2003) *Mandela Manuscript.* Mandela Centre of Memory.

Masuku, MT. (1998) *Rev JRL Rammala: A Case Study of an African Missionary.* University of South Africa.

Masuku, MT. (2010) *The Ministry of Beyers Naudé.* University of Pretoria.

Minaar, A. (1990) *The Great Depression 1929–1934 Adverse Exchange Rates and the South African Wool Farmer.* Taylor & Francis.

Mogotsi, G. (2022) *The Origin and Breakaway Groups of Barolong.* Mogotsi.

Mokoena, H. (2005) *The Making of a Kholwa Intellectual: A Discursive Biography of Magema Magwaza Fuze.* University of Cape Town.

Mokoena, H. (2009) *An Assembly of Readers: Magema Fuze and his Ilanga lase Natal Readers.* Journal of Southern African Studies.

Molumeli, J and Prum, M. (2015) *Missionary Work in Africa in Eugene Casalis's Time and Beyond.* Cambridge Scholars.

Murray, C. (1984) *Land, Power and Class in the Thaba Nchu District, Orange Free State, 1884–1983.* Taylor & Francis.

Ngcokovane, C. (1989) *The Demons of Apartheid. A moral and ethical analysis of the NGK, NP and Broederbond's justification of Apartheid.* Skotaville.

Nieftagodien, N and Gaule, S. (2012) *Orlando West, Soweto.* Wits University Press.

Pali, K. (2018) *An analysis of conflict situations within the leadership and various structures of the Dutch Reformed Church in Africa, Orange Free State.* HTS.

Peterson, B. (2000) *Monarchs, Missionaries and African Intellectuals: African Theatre and the Unmaking of Colonial Marginality.* Wits University Press.

Plaatje, S. (1982) *Native Life in South Africa.* Ravan Press.

Plaatjies Van Huffel, M. (2013) *The Belhar Confession: Born in the Struggle Against Apartheid in Southern Africa.* University of Stellenbosch.

Randall, P. (1982) *Not Without Honour: Tribute to Beyers Naudé.* Ravan Press.

Saayman, W. (2007) *Being Missionary, Being Human – An overview of Dutch Reformed Mission.* Cluster Publications.

Schoeman K (Ed.). (1987) *The Recollections of Elizabeth Rolland (1803–1901).* Human and Rousseau.

Setiloane, G. (1976) *The Image of God among the Sotho-Tswana*. Balkema.

Smith, A. (1940) *The Diary of Dr Andrew Smith*. The Van Riebeeck Society.

Smith, E. (1996) *The Mabilles of Basutoland*. Morija Museum & Archives.

Sundkler, B and Steed, C. (2000) *A History of the Church in Africa*. Cambridge University Press.

Thinane, TS. (2010) *The Institutionalisation of Effective Rehabilitation Programmes at Groenpunt Maximum Security Prison*. North West University.

Tlali, M. (1989) *Footprints in the Quag*. David Philip.

Van der Merwe, H. (1966) *Hosanna*. CLF.

Van Onselen, C. (1996) *The Seed Is Mine*. Jonathan Ball Publishers.

Watson, RL. (1977) *Missionary Influence at Thaba Nchu, 1833–1854: A Reassessment*. Boston University African Studies Center.

Watson, RL. (1980) *The Subjection of a South African State: Thaba Nchu, 1880–1884*. Cambridge University Press.

Wells, R. (1994) *An Introduction to the Music of Basotho*. Morija Museum and Archives.

Online

Barbara J Starmans. Retrieved from https://www.thesocialhistorian.com. Accessed on 28 November 2022.

Beyers Naudé profile. Retrieved from http://prominentpeople.co.za/naud-beyers.aspx. Accessed on 27 November 2019.

Coleman, G. Retrieved from https://www.sahistory.org.za/archive/gelukspan-hospital. Accessed on 28 November 2019.

DKW motorbike. Retrieved from https://en.wikipedia.org/wiki/DKW. Accessed on 1 November 2020.

Groenpunt Correctional Facility. Retrieved from https://www.enca.com/south-africa/groenpunt-prison-riot-management-flawed. Accessed on 10 November 2020.

Helwig D. Retrieved from http://www.rolling-inspiration-archives.co.za/content-archives/archive-article-details.php?paramID=279. Accessed on 1 December 2019.

James 'Sofasonke' Mpanza. Retrieved from https://www.sahistory.org.za/people/james-sofasonke-mpanza. Accessed on 13 January 2020.

Ma Plaatjies van Huffel. Retrieved from https://facebook.com/story.php?story_fbid=3987016525802&id. Accessed on 30 November 2022.

Mangcu, X. Retrieved from http://www.702.co.za/articles/246111/write-about-black-history-urges-xolela-mangcu. Accessed on 1 December 2019.

Masilela N. New African Movement. Retrieved from http://pzacad.pitzer.edu/NAM. Accessed on 29 September 2022.

Melanated Knowledge. Retrieved from Instagram (photos and videos from @melanatedknowledge). Accessed on 28 November 2022.

Reformed Family Forum. Retrieved from https://rff.christians.co.za/the-lesotho-evangelical-church-in-southern-africa-elcsa/. Accessed on 18 November 2020.

Stofberg Gedenkskool. Retrieved from https://af.wikipedia.org/wiki/Stofberg-gedenkskool. Accessed on 13 January 2020.

Tafira, K. Retrieved from https://www.google.com/amp/s/theconversation.com/amp/why-land-evokes-such-deep-emotions-in-africa-42125. Accessed on 10 November 2019.

Interviews

Reverend Boikanyo Modiboa – Pretoria East, Gauteng – 30 October 2019.

Dorcas Morobe – Bapong village, North West – 2 November 2019.

Ezekiel Lebotse – Uitkyk village, North West – 2 November 2019.

Dr Marthinus Bac – Pretoria, Gauteng – 4 December 2019.

Susan Sefatsa – Kroonstad, Free State – 5 December 2019.

Tsietsi Chapatso – Lindley, Free State – 6 December 2019.

Seetso Moremong – Setlopo village, North West – 17 December 2019.

Mmantlaletseng Morobe – Bapong village, North West – 18 December 2019.

Maki Tshabalala – Springbokpan village, North West – 18 December 2019.

Mampho Ntebele – Springbokpan village, North West – 18 December 2019.

Professor Takatso Mofokeng – Devon, Mpumalanga – 6 June 2020.

Tshidiso Mofokeng – Lotus Gardens, Gauteng – 8 October 2020.

Jerry Mofokeng – Thokoza, Gauteng – 12 October 2020.

Manosi Matona – Katlehong, Gauteng – 17 October 2020.

Rasebopela Mofokeng – Itsoseng – 20 December 2022.

Index

African Methodist Episcopal
  Church (AME Church) 21,
  46–47, 87, 206
African Morning Stars 51
Afrikaans 8, 20, 70, 74, 76, 89,
  121, 145, 185, 210
Ajayo, JF Ade 150
Amadodana ase Wesile 169
*Amagama Okuhlabelela
  (Dumisane)* 195
Anglican American Zulu Mission
  195
Anglican Church 156
Anglo-Boer War 22, 144
apartheid xi, 31, 48–49, 52,
  63, 67–68, 70, 75, 91, 107,
  143–144, 147, 157, 176–177,
  182, 184–185, 211
  see also segregation
Arbousset, Thomas xi, 19,
  134, 148, 151, 160, 166, 173,
  184–185
Arends, Aaron 131, 135
Ayandele, EA 150

Bac, Marthinus 71–72, 84–85
Bafokeng 14–17, 19, 39, 42, 205
Bakhatla 15
Bamaiyane 16
BaMakhoakhoa 15
Bamangwato 152
BaMoojane 14–15, 19–20
Bantu World 26
Barolong High School 106–107
Barorisi ba Morena 169
Basotho xii, 14–15, 19–20, 23,
  36, 39, 42, 51–52, 78, 110, 112,
  115, 124, 129–133, 135–136,
  139–142, 148, 151–152, 158,
  160–164, 167, 175–176, 188,
  191–194, 197–199, 201–202,
  204–206, 208–209
Basotho Cultural Village 209
Basutoland
  see Lesotho

Batlokoa 15, 20
BaTshele 14–15
Batswana 42, 79, 104, 150,
  152–153, 187
Beersheba xi, 129–131, 133–143,
  175, 180–181, 185, 187–189,
  192, 199
Beersheba Massacre 129–131,
  180, 182, 186
Beethoven, Ludwig van 196
Belhar Confession 42, 147
Bethesda Normal School 61
Biesiesvlei Mission Committee
  82
Black Consciousness 147
Black Jacks (police) 31, 34, 54
Black Power 147
Black Theology 147
Boesak, Allan 144
bohadi 162
Bolelang Taba Tsa Jesu (Tell the
  News of Jesus) 195
Bojosi, Dudu 79
Bojosi, Mapanana 79
Bongo Maffin 86
Bophuthatswana 71, 99, 126
Boshoff, Jacobus Nicolaas
  140–142
Boy Boy (nephew) 113
Brandwater river 16
Broederbond 144
Buti, Mohlomi 58
Buti, Mokheseng 58
Buti, Monyane 58
Buti, Palesa 58
Buti, Sam 58–59, 145, 174

cannibalism 16, 165–166
Casalis, Eugene xi, 134, 148,
  151, 153, 160, 164, 171, 173,
  176, 178, 184–185, 187, 191,
  194, 198
Chaane, Mahadi
  see Mofokeng (Chaane), Mahadi
Chaane, Makanono 37, 46

Chaane, Mamokgasi 37
Chaane, "Ou" Mmuso 22, 36–37,
  39–40, 44, 53–54, 125, 127
Chaane, Moifadi 37
Chaane, Thabiso 37
Chants de Sion 161, 164
Chapatso 13, 18, 23, 29, 76
Chapatso, Damara 114
Chapatso, Lekgowa 114
Chapatso, Tsietsi 108–111,
  113–114
Charles Velkes retailer 126
Christelike Vroue Vereeniging
  (CVV) 8, *116*, 119
Christianity 58, 109–113, 133,
  142, 148–150, 152–153,
  156–158, 160, 163, 168,
  177–178, 185, 191, 194, 198,
  206, 208
Coillard, François 160, 167,
  184, 188
Cole, Ernest 157
colonialism 22, 24, 31, 152, 155,
  161–163, 166, 177–178
Conference Missionnaire
  (Missionary Conference) 188
Coplan, David 137, 139–140, 160
Covid-19 24

Daumas, François 134, 136, 192
De Jager, Dr 79
De Klerk, BJ 166
Difaqane (Lifaqane) 15, 17, 150
Dihoja 20
Dikobe (Ou Dikobe) 67–70
Dlamini, Jacob 31
Dlamini, Nkileng Rose 36
dompas 31–32, 34, 43–44, 52, 54
Dreyer family 59
Dumisani hymnbook 159
Dutch East India Company 153
Dutch Reformed Church
  see NG Kerk

Eastern Brothers 51

222

Index 223

Eastern Leopards 50
EFF (Economic Freedom Fighters) 100
Ekurhuleni 32, 34
Ellenberger, Frederic 14–17, 19
Emmarentia Geldenhuys School 61
Emmarentia High School 70, 105–107
Enlightenment 178
Expedition for Exploring Central Africa 117

Fanon, Frantz 162
Ferreira, Ms (Mejuffrou) 8
Ferreira, TI 4, 8, 68, 75, 79, 99
Frazer, Dominee 175
Free State–Basotho War 139, 188

Gelukspan vii, ix–xi, xiii, 1–2, 4, 5, 7, 35, 60, 66, 67–72, 74–76, 78–79, 80, 83–86, 87–88, 92–93, 98–99, 101, 103–107, 110, 116, 119, 121–122
George Goch 38, 51
Germiston Station 24–26
Goch, George 38
Gold Standard 33
Goodall, Norman 57
Gosselin, Constand xi, 148, 151, 160, 173, 198
GPO Sweepers 52
Grahamstown Journal 20
Gray, Robert 156
Great Depression 33
Grey, George 141
Groenpunt Maximum Correctional Facility 63
Group Areas Act 36, 61

Handel, George Frideric 160, 196
Haverman, Johannes 155
Haydn, Joseph 159–160, 196
Helpmekaar 144
Heyns, Flip 37, 58
Hip Hop Pantsula 118
Hlabeli 15–16
Hofmeyr, AM 56
Hosanna hymnbook 125, 146, 158–159, 173–174, 194, 196
House of Bondage 157
Hymn 12 (Rolland) 172
Hymn 53 (Casalis) 173
Hymn 89 (Rolland) 168
Hymn 108 (Casalis) 171
Hymn 111 ('Ke Na Le Molisa', Rolland) 169–170
Imperial Air Force 52

imperialism 152, 162–163, 165, 177
Incwadi Yamaculo hymnbook 159
initiation 109, 111, 114, 152, 160, 162–163
International Missionary Council 57
Introduction to the Music of Basotho 194
IPCC 169
Islam 149

Jackson, Mary 135
Jandrell, LHM 159
Janse van Rensburg, Nelis 180
'Jehova Molimo oa Iseraele' 164–165
Johannesburg Bantu Football Association (JBFA) 50
John Paul II 208
'Jo Lefifi Le Lekaakang' 167
Jordan, Gerrit 191–194
Joyous Celebration 169, 190, 195
July, Robert 178

Kabza De Small 118
Kadalie, Clements 58
Kaizer Chiefs 49
Kama, Chief 153
Ke Lesitsi, Ke Tla Feela (I'm Mournful, I Come Empty) 195
Kereke ya Fora (Church of the French) xii, 42, 140, 143, 173–175, 180, 184, 210
Kgobokoe (young leader) 54
Khama rulers 152
Khati, Thekiso 161
'Khawuleza' 45
Khotso 17
Khuli Chana 118
Koeema (Kueeme) 13, 15
Koko, Mrs 4–6
Kritzinger, Klippies (JNJ) 56–57, 62–63
Kruger, Paul 141
Kueeme (Koeema) 13, 15

Lala Ho Nna 195
Lebona (cousin of Mongangane) 54
Lebotse, Ezekiel 83, 90, 97, 99–102, 105
Lebotse, Hilda 105
LECSA
 see Lesotho Evangelical Church of Southern Africa
Lekalake, CN 106
Lekula la Matlere 110

Lephakga, Tshepo 176–177
le Réveil 186
Leselinyana la Lesotho 15, 195, 198
Leshota, Paul 161–166
Lesotho (Basutoland) vii, ix, xii, 14–15, 20, 22, 27, 42, 78, 177, 139, 160–161, 164–165, 175, 181–184, 188, 191, 194–195, 197–200, 204, 206–209, 211–213
Lesotho Evangelical Church of Southern Africa (LECSA) 182–183, 206–207
Letsosa, Rantoa 166
Letuka Hlabeli 15–17
Libertas 21–22, 36, 39–40, 54, 58
'Lichaba Tsohle Tsa Lefatshe' 166–167
Lichtenburg Reserve 82, 88, 94, 104
Lifela tsa Sione ('Hymns of Zion') hymn book 78, 125, 159–161, 164, 166, 170, 173, 182, 187–188, 191, 193–195, 199
Livingstone, David 152–153, 166
London Missionary Society 150, 152, 186
Lotlhakane village 13, 93, 116–118, 127, 211
Louw, AA 181
Lucky 7 specials 126–127
Ludorf, Monsieur 187

Mabille, Adolphe 15, 160, 195, 198
Mabula 15–17
Madieleng, Johannes 33
Maeder, Fritz 193
Mafa, Lebohang 200, 204, 212
Magogogong 28, 31–33, 38
Maguire, Richard 49, 52
Mahlangu, Thomas 57, 62
Mahlatsai 14
Mahlatsi 14
Maile, ML 62
Makeba, Miriam 45
Malan, César 161, 164, 191
Mandela, Nelson xiii, 43
Mankejane 17
Marabi-style 26, 28
MaRampa (nurse) 79
Maree, LP 56
Marokane, Dominee 99
Masekela, Hugh 28
Masekoane 16
Mashaba, Winnie 169, 190
Masilela, Ntongela 151

Masithela, Limpho 212
Masithela, Tsepo 206
Masopha 15
Masuka, Dorothy 45
Matebele 14
Mathebetoa 17
Matsoso 17
MBB
  see Mokgatlo wa Badumedi ba Bakreste
Mel, Conrad 155
Methodist Church 21, 93, 153, 195, 199, 213
migrant labour 28, 31, 52, 182
missionaries xi, 14, 19, 21–22, 26, 53, 56–57, 74–75, 77, 87–88, 104, 112, 116, 129–130, 132–137, 139–140, 146, 148, 150–153, 155, 157–158, 160–165, 167–169, 174–178, 180–182, 184–186, 188–194, 198–199, 205–208
  see also Moroka Missionary Institution; London Missionary Society; Paris Evangelical Mission Society; Anglican American Zulu Mission
Mkwanazi, Andries 'Pele Pele' 50
Mmaausi 118
Moboleli oa Litaba ('The Clarion') 137, 187, 199
Moeletsi, Chief 142
Moepeng, Shadrack x
Moffat, Robert 150, 152–153, 160, 186
Mofokeng, Bernard 13, 37, 44–45, 54–55, 72, 143
Mofokeng, Chapatso 3, 211
Mofokeng, Lesley ix, xiii, 1
Mofokeng, Madibuseng 113
Mofokeng (Chaane), Mahadi vii, xi, 2, 7–8, 10, 35–37, 39–41, 45, 47, 53–54, 58–59, 72, 116, 118–128, 214
Mofokeng, Mahali 3, 211
Mofokeng, Mapiletsa 39–40, 72
Mofokeng, Mongangane Wilfred vii, ix–xiii, 2–3, 4–7, 10–11, 13, 18–23, 26–32, 40–41, 46–52, 54–56, 58, 60–62, 72–73, 75–77, 79–84, 87–99, 101, 103, 107–114, 118–119, 122, 143, 146, 189, 200, 210, 212, 214
Mofokeng, Moses Teboho 13, 41, 47, 54–55, 58, 70, 72, 74, 83, 143, 200–201, 214

Mofokeng, Motswantweng Ephraim (Spanky) 13, 26–27, 29, 38, 44, 46, 55, 58–59, 72, 74, 76, 78, 83, 100, 103, 123, 143
Mofokeng, Mpho 41
Mofokeng, Seabata 23
Mofokeng, Selloane 18–19, 109
Mofokeng, Takatso (father of Mongangane) 13, 21, 30, 41, 87, 113, 200
Mofokeng, Takatso (son of Mongangane) 41–48, 54–61, 68–72, 74–79, 83, 87, 100, 103–107, 109–113, 120, 123, 140, 142–143, 147–148, 173–174
Mofokeng, Thabo Makuoe Jerry 13, 35–37, 39–41, 44, 54, 72, 88, 143
Mofokeng, Tshidiso 13, 70, 72, 89, 108, 118, 121
Mohapeloa, Polumo 195
Moholo, Solly 190
Mokgatlo wa Badumedi ba Bakreste (MBB) 8, 53, 93
Mokgosinyana, Bethuel 50
Mokhachane 16–17
Mokhukhu, ZCC 169
Mokiba 16–17
Mokoena brothers 99
Molamu, Shepstone 79, 126
Molamu, Susan Nkeng 79
Molimo ke Moea (God is a Spirit) 195
Molopo reserve 75
Montlha 13
Mooi, Chief 142
Moojane (born 1690) 13, 17
Moojane (born 1710) 13
Morallana 16
Morapedi, Dorothy 4, 125
Moremong, Seetso ix, 88–89, 91, 93, 95, 97–101
Morija (*Letsha la Thuto*) 151, 159, 182, 185–186, 198–199, 212
Morobe, Jasi 93
Morobe, Mabuti 104
Morobe, Mantlaletseng 82, 92, 94, 97, 101, 104, 116
Moroka Missionary Institution 21, 26
Moroka Swallows 51
Moshoeshoe I xii, 15–17, 20, 117, 129–130, 139–142, 148, 151–153, 174–176, 180, 184, 188, 198, 200–201, 202, 204–209

Moshoeshoe II 201
'Mote, Ramatseatsana 198, 207
Mothobi, Dominee 99
Motsamai 27
Motsatse, Fred 21–22, 46
Motsatse, Teacher 21–22, 46
Motsweding FM 118
Mount Kgoele 17–19
Mpanza, James Sofasonke 43, 51
Murray, Andrew 155
Mzilikazi 75, 186

Naha 29–30, 38
Nanau 13
Napier, George 129
National House of Traditional and Khoisan Leaders (NHTKL) 118
Native (Bantu) Trusts xi, 66–69, 75, 78, 86, 107
Native Land Act, 1913 22, 66
Native Trust and Land Act No. 18, 1936 66, 75
Naudé, Beyers 145
Ndezel' Uncedo 195
Nederduitse Gereformeerde Kerk
  see NG Kerk
New African Movement 151
Newclare ('Sdikidiki') 38–39, 50
NG Kerk (Nederduitse Gereformeerde Kerk, Dutch Reformed Church) xi, 2, 19–22, 42–43, 46–47, 53, 55–57, 61, 63, 74, 80, 84, 93, 119, 125, 143–145, *146*–148, 154, 157–159, 174–177, 180–186, 195–196, 210
NG Kerk in Afrika (Black NG Kerk) 21, 42, 55, 63, 74, 144, 147, 158–159, 174–176, 180–182, 195–196
NG Kerk, General Synod 8, 159
NG Sendingkerk (Dutch Reformed Mission Church) 42, 63, 144, 147, 155, 181
Nicol, William 145
Nielsen, Eric W 57
Nkejane 13–16, 18
North West University xiii
Notshi 118
Ntabenyane 16
Nthakge, Moruti 174
Ntoyi (Swallows patron) 51
Ntsala family 113–114
Ntwane, Moruti 174

Odendaal, AA 56
Oosthuysen, JC 159

Index 225

Orlando x, 40–41, 43–44, *45–46*, 48–49, 51, 54, 60, 74, 78, 90, 105
Orlando Pirates 48–50
Orlando Shelters 40, 44, 48, 54, 105

Paris Evangelical Mission Society (PEMS) 15, 129, 175, 181–183, 185, 195, 188
Pellissier, Jean Pierre 134
PEMS
 see Paris Evangelical Mission Society
Peterson, Bhekizizwe 178
Phalane Council (Committee) *87*, 90–91
Phalime, Raphael 33
Phillip, John 150
Plaatjies-van Huffel, Mary-Anne 8
polygamy 134, 162–163, 198
Pretoria University 56
Pretorius, Andries 141
Princeton University 105
'Progress Towards Health For All in the Gelukspan Health Ward – 1985' 71

Qiloane 205, 208
 see also Thaba Bosiu

Ramaiyane 16
Ramatseatsana rock 207
Ramothibe, Lydia 93, 104
Ramothibe, Ntate 104–105, 107
Rand Airport 34
Rapetloane, Filemone 195
Ratlali 14
Recollections of Elizabeth Rolland (1803 to 1901), The 189–190
Reitsositse Primary School 91
Religious Tract Society 159, 195
Retief, Piet 18–20
Rolland, Catherine 189
Rolland, Elise 189
Rolland, Elizabeth 131–136, 139, 141, 161, 187–189
Rolland, Emile 188–189
Rolland, Samuel 129–139, 141–142, 161, 168–170, 172, 175, 180, 184–188, 191, 194–195, 199
Roman Catholic Church 156

Santho, Evangelist 46
Sauer, Johannes 140, 180
Save Alexandra Campaign 145
Seate, Tshepo (Stoan) 86

Seatlholo, Tebogo 118
seBersheeba 189–190
Sechaba 169
Sechele rulers 152
Sefatsa, Masabata 36–37, 40, 121
segregation viii, 33, 68, 76, 148, 186
Sekese, Azariel 14–15
Sekgobela, Lebo 169, 190
Sekonyela 20, 142
seliba sa 'MaMohato (the well of 'MaMohato) xii, 202–*203*, 204
Sello, A 195
Sendinginstituut 56
Senekal, Frederik 19
Sepenya 13
Sesotho 20, 24, 39, 78, 112, 125, 131, 137, 159–160, 164, 182, 187, 193–195, 199, 209–210
Setlagole reserve 75
Setswana 70, 78, 104, 118, 131, 150, 159, 186, 193–195, 199, 204
Shadi's General Dealer 127
Shaka 14
Sharpeville Massacre 106
Smith, Andrew 117
Smith, Harry 174
Sophiatown 38, 50–51
South African Clothing Workers Union 33
Soweto Gospel Choir 169
Stellenbosch University 56–57
'Stimela' 28
Stoan
 see Seate, Tshepo
Stockenström, Andries 20, 130
Stockholm syndrome 144
Stofberg-Gedenkskool (Stofberg Memorial School, Seminary) 36, 54–55, 57, 59–64, 74, 78–79, 112, 123
Stofberg, Pieter 56
Streak (shopkeeper) 68, 70, 79

Tambo, Oliver 43
Tema, SS 62
Thaba Bosiu xii, 117, 148, 151, 173, 185, *197*–198, 200, *202*, 205–206, 208–209, 212
Themere 13
Thethana river 19
Thokoza 29, 35–36
Tholo, Ntate 91, *96*
Tlali, Miriam 38–39
Tlamelang Special School 4, 84, 120
Tontshi 13
Tracey, Hugh 192

traditional practices and customs 24, 29, 37, 39, 44, 75, 108–112, 115, 118–119, 123, 127, 129, 152, 163, 176–177, 192, 208
translation of Bible, hymns viii, 150–151, 159–160, 164, 166, 187, 194–195, 199, 210
Tseana 14
Tseele 16
Tshehlo 13–20
Tshokolo (cousin of Jerry Mofokeng) 37
Tshola, Tshepo 169, 206
Tsietso 13, 15
Tuks Senganga 118
Turfloop (University of Limpopo) 105, 174
Twala, Ntate 89, 103

Uitkyk Primary School 91–92
Uniting Reformed Church in Southern Africa (URCSA) 42, 57, 63, 109, 143, 145–*146*, 147–148, 159, 164, 173, *183*, 186, 189–190, 213
University of Lesotho 161
University of the Witwatersrand (Wits) ix, xiii
URCSA
 see Uniting Reformed Church in Southern Africa

Van der Kemp, JT 150
Van der Merwe, HCS 159
Van der Wall, Dominee 175
Van der Watt, Gideon 180–182, 184
Van Lier, Helperus 154
Van Niekerk, AS 56
Van Wyk, JA 56
Verwoerd, Hendrik 64
Victoria 152
Voortrekkers 18, 156
Vos, Michiel 154

Warden, Henry Douglas 130
Webber, David 204
Wells, Robin 115, 194
World War I 34, 144
World War II 88

Xaluva, W 62

Zietsman, BW 159

About the author

Lesley Lehlohonolo Mofokeng is a former journalist, author and media specialist based in Johannesburg. He has worked for *Sunday Times*, *City Press* and *Sowetan* and is a popular culture commentator on radio stations such as Metro FM, YFM, Motsweding FM, Kaya FM as well as several TV shows. Mofokeng's first book was the best-selling biography *Bitch! Please. I'm Khanyi Mbau* (2012) and he has authored and edited several other biographies, a recipe book and a collection of essays. He obtained his BA Communication (Honours) from North West University and holds a Master of Arts degree from the University of Witwatersrand, Johannesburg.

www.ingramcontent.com/pod-product-compliance
Lightning Source LLC
Chambersburg PA
CBHW072342090426
42741CB00012B/2892